SAY
POLISH

BY
VICTOR RAYSMAN

SECOND EDITION

DOVER PUBLICATIONS, INC.
NEW YORK

Bibliographical Note

Say It In Polish is a new work, first published by Dover
Publications, Inc., in 1955.

International Standard Book Number: 0-486-20808-

Manufactured in the United States of America
Dover Publications, Inc., 31 East 2nd Street,
Mineola, N.Y. 11501

TABLE OF CONTENTS

SCHEME OF PRONUNCIATION

VOWELS

It must be remembered that in Polish, as in Italian, Spanish, and the other Slavic languages, the vowels are pure, consisting of one sound only and not drawled as is often the case in English. The following equivalents should be applied consistently:

ah as in *father*.
e or *eh* as in *met*.
ay as in *say*.
ie as in *die*.
ee as in *meet*.
o or *oh* as in *note*.
i or *ih* as in *fit*.
ow as in *cow*.

CONSONANTS

Most of the consonants are to be read as in English, but with the following modifications or suggestions:

kh as in *loch* (Scottish) or *ach* (German).
r is trilled with the tip of the tongue.
y as in *yes*. NOTE: Syllables like *kyeh*, *nyeh*, *pyeh* will occur from time to time. Be careful to retain the quality of *y* as in *yes*, and to pronounce only one syllable.

ch as in *church*.

sh as in *show*.

zh like the *s* in *measure*.

dzh like the *j* in *jam*.

shch as in *fresh cheese*. The spelling looks
complex, but the sound is the same as in
English.

PALATALS

The palatals are indicated by a line above
the letters. There are no exact equivalents in
English for these sounds, but you will be under-
stood if you say *ch*, *sh*, and *zh* instead of $\overline{ch}$, $\overline{sh}$,
and $\overline{zh}$. The sounds are properly produced,
however, with the tip of the tongue touching
the lower teeth and the middle of the tongue
pressed near the alveolar ridge, just above the
upper teeth. The best way to learn these
sounds is by imitating a native speaker or by
listening to a record.

$\overline{ch}$ like the *t* in *nature* or *not yet*.

$\overline{sh}$ like *sh*, but palatalized (German: *ich*).

$d\overline{zh}$ like the *d* in *verdure* or *mid-year*.

$\overline{zh}$ like *zh*, but palatalized.

$\overline{n}$ as in *onion* or the first *n* in *mañana*
(Spanish). (When this occurs in the
middle of a word, it is transcribed *ny*, as
in *canyon*.)

Syllables that are printed in capital letters are
to be stressed. *M.* and *F.* refer to masculine

and feminine. Sentences that are to be addressed only to a man are preceded by *to M*. To address the same statement to a woman, substitute the word *pani* (PAH-nyih) for *pan*. Where there is no indication of gender, the phrases may be addressed to or used by persons of either sex.

NOTE: In order to facilitate revision of the text for future editions, a few numbers have been skipped between major divisions. These interruptions in the numbering of the phrases do not indicate omissions in the text.

USEFUL EXPRESSIONS
WYRAZENIA POTOCZNE

1. Yes. No. Perhaps.
Tak. Nie. Może.
tahk. nyeh. MO-zheh.

2. Please. Excuse me.
Proszę. Przepraszam.
PRO-sheh. psheh-PRAH-shahm.

3. Thanks (very much).
Dziękuje (bardzo).
djen-KOO-yeh. (BAHR-dzoh).

4. You are welcome.
Bardzo proszę.
BAHR-dzoh PRO-sheh.

5. Do you speak English?
(*to M.*) Czy pan mówi po angielsku?
chih pahn MOO-vee po ahn-GYEL-skoo?

6. I speak only (English, French).
Mówię tylko po (angielsku, francusku).
MOO-vyeh TIL-ko po (ahn-GYEL-skoo, frahn-TSOO-skoo).

7. German. Italian.
Niemiecku. Włosku.
nyeh-MYEH-tskoo. VWO-skoo.

8. I am from the United States.
Jestem z Ameryki.
YES-tem z ah-MEH-ri-kee.

9. My (mailing) address is ——.
Mój adres jest ——.
moo-ee AH-dress yest——.

10. (He, she) is from ——.
(On, ona) jest z ——.
(ohn, OH-nah) yest z ——.

11. Please speak more slowly.
Proszę mówić wolniej.
PRO-sheh MOO-veech VOL-nyay.

12. I (do not) understand.
(Nie) Rozumiem.
(nyeh) ro-ZOO-myehm.

13. Repeat it, please.
Proszę powtórzyć.
PRO-sheh pohv-TOO-zhich.

14. Again.   Also.
Jeszcze raz.   Także.
YESH-cheh rahz.   TAHK-zheh.

15. Write it down, please.
Proszę napisać.
PRO-sheh nah-PEE-sach.

16. What do you wish?
(*to M.*) Czego pan sobie życzy?
CHE-goh pahn SOH-byeh ZHIH-chih?

17. How much is it?
Ile to kosztuje?
EE-leh toh kohsh-TOO-yeh?

18. Come in.
Proszę wejść.
PRO-sheh VAY͞SH-ch̄.

19. Wait a moment.
Proszę zaczekać chwilę.
PRO-sheh zah-CHEH-kah͞ch̄ KHVEE-leh.

20. Why? When?
Dlaczego? Kiedy?
dlah-CHEH-goh? KYEH-dih?

21. How? How long?
Jak? Jak długo?
yahk? yahk DWOO-goh?

22. How far? Who? What?
Jak daleko? Kto? Co?
yahk dah-LEH-koh? ktoh? tsoh?

23. Where (is, are) ——?
Gdzie (jest, są) ——?
gd͞zheh (yest, sohn)——?

24. Washroom or toilet (for either sex).
Toaleta.
toh-ah-LEH-tah.

25. Here. There.
Tu. Tam.
too. tahm.

26. It is (not) all right.
To (nie) jest w porządku.
toh (nyeh) yest v por-ZHONT-koo.

27. It is (old, new).
To jest (stare, nowe).
toh yest (STAH-reh, NO-veh).

28. Empty. Full.
Puste. Pełne.
POO-steh. PEHW-neh.

29. That is (not) all.
To (nie) wszystko.
toh (nyeh) VSHIST-koh.

30. From *or* with.
Do. Z *or* ze (when the following word
    begins with two consonants).
doh. z or zeh.

31. In. On. Near. Far.
W. Na: Blisko. Daleko.
v. nah. BLEES-koh. dah-LEH-ko.

32. In front of. Behind.
Z przodu. Z tyłu.
z PSHOH-doo. z TIH-woo.

33. Beside. Inside. Outside.
Obok. Wewnątrz. Nazewnątrz.
O-bohk. VEV-nohnch. nah-ZEHV-nontch.

34. Something. Nothing.
Coś. Nic.
t̲osh. neets.

35. Many. Few.
Wiele. Parę.
VYEH-leh. PAH-reh.

36. (Much) more, less.
(Dużo) więcej, mniej.
(*DOO-zhoh*) *VYEN-tsay, mnyay.*

37. (A little) more, less.
(Trochę) więcej, mniej.
(*TRO-heh*) *VYEN-tsay, mnyay.*

38. Enough. Too much.
Dosyć. Za dużo.
DOH-sĭch. zah DOO-zhoh.

39. Much. Many.
Dużo. Wiele.
DOO-zho. VYEH-ļeh.

40. Good. Better (than).
Dobrze. Lepiej (niż).
DOB-zheh. LEH-pyay (neezh).

41. Bad. Worse (than).
Źle. Gorzej (niż).
zhleh. GO-zhay (neezh).

42. Now. Immediately.
Teraz. Natychmiast.
TEH-rahz. nah-TIKH-myahst.

43. Soon. Later.
Zaraz. Później.
ZAH-rahz. POOZH-nyay.

44. As soon as possible.
Jak najszybciej.
yahk nie-SHIB-chay.

45. At the latest.   At least.
Najpóźniej.   Przynajmniej.
nie-POO͞ZH-nyay.   pshih-NIE-mnyay.

46. It is (too) late.
Jest (za) późno.
yest (zah) POO͞ZH-no.

47. It is early.
Wcześnie.
VCHE͞SH-nyeh.

48. Slow.   Slower.
Wolno.   Wolniej.
VOHL-noh.   VOHL-nyay.

49. Quickly.   Faster.
Szybko.   Szybciej.
SHIB-ko   SHIB-c͞hay.

50. I am (not) in a hurry.
Ja się (nie) śpieszę.
yah s͞heh (nyeh) S͞HPYEH-sheh.

51. I am (warm, cold).
Jest mi (gorąco, zimno).
yest mee (go-ROHN-tso, ͞ZHEEM-no).

52. I am (hungry, thirsty, sleepy).
(*M.*) Jestem głodny, spragniony, senny.
YES-tem GWOD-nih, sprah-GNYO-nih. SEN-nih.

53. Busy.   Tired.   Ill.   Lost.
(*M.*) Zajęty.   Zmęczony.   Chory.
Zabłądziłem.
*zah-YEN-tih.   zmen-CHO-nih.   KHO-rih.
zah-bwohn-D͞ZHEE-wem.*

54. What is the matter here?
Co się stało?
tso sheh STAH-woh?

55. Help! Fire! Thief!
Pomocy! Pożar! Złodziej!
po-MO-tsih! PO-zhahr! ZWO-dzhay!

56. Look out!
Uważaj!
oo-VAH-zhie!

57. Listen. Look here.
Słuchaj. Patrz.
SWOO-khie. pahtch.

58. Can you (help, tell) me ——?
Proszę mi (pomóc, powiedzieć) ——.
PRO-sheh mee (PO-moots, po-VYEH-dzhech)
——.

59. I am looking for ——.
Szukam ——.
SHOO-kahm ——.

60. I should like ——.
(*M.*) Chciałbym ——.
h-CHOW-bim ——.

61. Can you recommend ——?
(*to M.*) Czy pan może polecić ——?
chih pahn MOH-zheh po-LEH-cheech ——?

62. Do you want ——?
(*to M.*) Czy pan chce ——?
chih pahn h-TSE ——?

63. I am (glad, sorry).
(*M.*) Jestem (zadowolony, zmartwiony).
YES-tem (zah-do-vo-LO-nih, zmart-VYO-nih).

64. It is (not) my fault.
To (nie) moja wina.
toh (nyeh) mo-yah VEE-nah.

65. Whose fault is it?
Czyja to wina?
CHI-yah toh VEE-nah?

66. I (do not) know.
(Nie) wiem.
(nyeh) vyem.

67. I (do not) think so.
Ja tak (nie) sądzę.
yah tahk (nyeh) SOHN-dzeh.

68. What is that for?
Po co to?
poh tso toh?

69. What is this called in Polish?
Jak to się nazywa po polsku?
yahk toh sheh nah-ZIH-vah poh POHL-skoo?

70. How do you say ——?
Jak się wymawia ——?
yahk sheh vih-MAH-vyah ——?

71. How do you spell ——?
Jak się pisze ——?
yahk sheh PEE-sheh ——?

DIFFICULTIES
TRUDNOŚCI

74. I cannot find my hotel address.
Nie mogę znaleźć mojego hotelu.
*nyeh MOH-geh znah-LESH-che moh-YEH-goh
ho-TEH-loo.*

75. I do not remember the street.
Nie pamiętam nazwy ulicy.
nyeh pah-MYEN-tahm NAHZ-vih oo-LEE-tsih.

76. I have lost my friend.
(*M.*) Zgubiłem mojego znajomego.
zgoo-BEE-wem mo-YEH-go znah-yo-MEH-go.

77. I left my (purse, wallet) ——.
(*M.*) Zostawiłem moją (torbę, portfel)
——.
*zos-tah-VEE-wem MOH-yohn (TOR-beh,
PORT-fehl) ——.*

78. I forgot my (money, keys).
(*M.*) Zapomniałem (pieniądze, klucze).
*zah-pom-NYAH-wem (pyeh-NYON-dze,
KLOO-cheh).*

79. I have missed my (train, plane, bus).
(*M.*) 'Spóźniłem się na (pociąg, samolot,
autobus).
*spoozh-NEE-wem sheh nah (POH-chong, sah-
MOH-lot, ow-TOH-booss).*

80. What am I to do?
Co mam zrobić?
tsoh mahm ZROH-beech?

81. You said it would cost ——.
(*to M.*) Pan powiedział że to kosztuje ——.
pahn poh-VYEH-dzhow zheh toh kohsh-TOO-yeh ——.

82. They are bothering (me, us).
Oni (mnie, nam) przeszkadzają.
OH-nee (mnyeh, nahm) psheh-shkah-DZAH-yohn).

83. Go away.
Odejdź.
O-daych.

84. I will call the police.
Zawołam policję.
zah-VOH-wahm po-LEE-tsyeh.

85. Where is the police station?
Gdzie jest stacja policyjna?
gdzheh yest STAHTS-yah po-lee-TSIH-nah?

86. I have been robbed of ——.
Okradziono mnie.
o-krah-DZHOH-noh mn-YEH.

87. The lost and found desk.
Biuro znalezionych rzeczy.
BYOO-roh znah-leh-ZHOH-nikh ZHEH-chih.

GREETINGS
PRZYWITANIA

90. Good morning.   Good evening.
Dzień dobry.   Dobry wieczór.
dzhen DOH-brih.   DOH-brih VYEH-choor.

91. Hello.   Good-bye.
Halo.   Dowidzenia.
HAH-loh.   do-veed-ZEN-yah.

92. My name is Smith.
Nazywam się Smith.
nah-ZIH-vahm sheh Smith.

93. What is your name?
(*to M.*) Jak się pan nazywa?
yahk sheh pahn nah-ZIH-vah?

94. May I introduce (Mr., Mrs., Miss) ——?
Proszę poznać (Pana, Panią, Pannę) ——?
*PRO-sheh POZ-nahch (PAH-nah, PAH-nyohn,
PAH-neh) ——?*

95. My wife.   My husband.
Moja żona.   Mój mąż
MOH-yah ZHO-nah.   MOO-ee mohnzh.

96. My daughter.   My son.
Moja córka.   Mój syn.
MO-yah TSOOR-kah.   MOO-ee sin.

97. My friend.
Mój znajomy.
MOO-ee znah-YO-mih.

98. My sister.   My brother.
Moja siostra.   Mój brat.
MO-yah SHOS-trah.   MOO-ee braht.

99. How are you?
Jak się pan ma?
yahk sheh pahn mah?

100. How is your family?
Jak się ma rodzina?
yahk sheh mah roh-DZHEE-nah?

101. (Not) very well.
(Nie) bardzo dobrze.
(nyeh) BAHR-dzo DOB-zhe.

102. Please sit down.
Proszę usiąść.
PRO-sheh oo-SHONSH-ch.

103. I have enjoyed myself very much.
Bardzo mi było przyjemnie.
BAHR-dzo mee BI-woh pshi-YEM-nyeh.

104. I hope to see you again soon.
Mam nadzieję że się zobaczymy wkrótce.
mahm nah-DZHEE-yeh zheh sheh zo-bah-CHI-mi VKROO-tse.

105. Come to see me.
Proszę mnie odwiedzić.
PRO-sheh mn-YEH od-VYEH-dzheech.

106. Give me your address (and telephone number).
Proszę dać mi swój adres (i numer telefonu).
PRO-sheh dahch mee svooy AHD-res (ee NOO-mer teh-leh-FO-noo).

107. Give my regards to ——.
Proszę pozdrowić ——.
PRO-sheh poh-ZDRO-veech ——.

108. We are traveling to ——.

Jedziemy do ——.

ye-DZHE-mih doh ——.

TRAVEL: GENERAL EXPRESSIONS
W PODRÓŻY

112. I want to go to the airline office.

Chcę pójść do biura linii lotniczej.

*htseh pooeeshch doh BYOO-rah LEE-nee lot-
ÑEE-chay.*

113. Where is the ——?

Gdzie jest ——?

gdzheh yest——?

114. The airport.   The bus station.

Lotnisko.   Stacja autobusowa.

*lot-ÑEES-ko.   STAH-tsyah ow-to-boo-SOH-
vah.*

115. The dock.   The railroad station.

Dok.   Stacja kolejową.

dohk.   STAH-tsyah ko-leh-YOH-vah.

116. How long will it take me to go to ——?

Jak długo jedzie się do ——?

yahk DWOO-go YEH-dzhe sheh do ——?

117. When will we arrive ——?

Kiedy przyjedziemy do ——?

KYEH-dih pshih-yeh-DZHEH-mih do ——?

118. Please get me a taxi.

Proszę mi zawołać taksówke.

*PRO-sheh mee zah-VOH-wahch tahk-SOOV-
keh.*

119. The ticket office.
Kasa biletowa.
KAH-sah bee-le-TO-vah.

120. A ticket.   A timetable.
Bilet.   Rozkład jazdy.
BEE-let.   ROS-kwahd YAHZ-dih.

121. A porter.   The check room.
Bagażowy.   Przechowalnia.
bah-gah-ZHOH-vih.   pshe-kho-VAL-nyah.

122. The platform.
Peron.
PEH-ron.

123. Is this seat taken?
Czy to miejsce jest zajęte?
chi toh MYAYS-tseh yest zah-YEN-teh?

124. Can I reserve a seat?
Czy mogę zarezerwować miejsce?
*chi MO-geh · zah-re-zer-VO-vahch MYAYS-
tseh?*

125. A seat near the window.
Miejsce przy oknie.
MYAYS-tseh pshih OK-nyeh.

126. Is this the (direct) way to ——?
Czy to jest (bezpośrednia) droga do ——?
*chih toh yest (bez-poh-SHRED-nya) DROH-
gah doh ——?*

127. How does one go (there)?
Jak się (tam) jedzie?
yahk sheh (tahm) YEH-dzheh?

128. Where do I turn?
Gdzie mam skręcić?
gdźheh mahm SKREN-c̄heec̄h?

129. To the north.   To the south.
Na północ.   Na południe.
nah POOW-nots.   nah poh-WOOD-nyeh.

130. To the west.   To the east.
Na zachód.   Na wschód.
nah ZAH-hood.   nah VS-khood.

131. To the right.   To the left.
Na prawo.   Na lewo.
nah PRAH-voh.   nah LEH-voh.

132. Straight ahead.
Prosto naprzód.
PROHS-toh NAHP-shood.

133. Forward.   Back.
Naprzód.   W tył.
NAHP-shood.   V till.

134. Street.   Place.
Ulica.   Plac.
oo-LEE-tsa.   plahts.

135. Please point.
Proszę mi wskazać.
PROH-sheh mee VSKAH-zahc̄h.

136. Do I have to change?
Czy mam się przesiąść?
chi mahm s̄heh PSHE-shonshch?

AT THE CUSTOMS
W KOMORZE CELNEJ

138. This is my baggage.
To jest mój bagaż.
toh yest MOO-ee BAH-gazh.

139. Here is my passport.   Permit.
Mój paszport.   Przepustka.
MOO-y PASH-pohrt.   pshe-POOST-kah.

140. Shall I open everything?
Czy mam otworzyć wszystko?
chi mahm oht-VOH-zhich VSHIST-koh?

141. I cannot open that.
Nie mogę tego otworzyć.
nyeh MOH-geh TEH-go oht-VOH-zhich.

142. I have nothing to declare.
Nie mam nic do oclenia.
nyeh mahm neets do ohts-LEH-nyah.

143. I have lost my key.
Zgubiłem klucz.
zgoo-BEE-wem klooch.

144. All this is for my personal use.
To wszystko jest do osobistego użytku.
toh   VSHIST-koh yest doh oh-soh-bees-TEH-go oo-ZHIT-koo.

145. There is nothing here but ——.
Tam niema nic, prócz ——.
tahm NYE-mah neets, prooch ——.

146. These are gifts.
To są prezenty.
toh sohn preh-ZEHN-tih.

147. Are these things dutiable?
Czy te rzeczy należy oclić?
chih teh ZHE-chih nah-LEH-zhih OTS-leech?

148. How much must I pay?
Ile mam zapłacić?
EE-leh mahm za-PWAH-cheech?

149. This is all I have.
To jest wszystko co mam.
toh yest VSHIST-ko tso mahm.

150. Please be careful.
Ostrożnie, proszę!
ohst-ROZH-nyeh, PRO-sheh!

151. Have you finished?
(*to M.*) Czy pan skończył?
chih pahn SKOHN-chill?

152. I cannot find my baggage.
Nie mogę znaleźć bagażu.
nyeh MOH-geh ZNAH-lesh-ch bah-GAH-zhoo.

153. My train leaves in —— minutes.
Mój pociąg odchodzi za —— minut.
*MOO-ee PO-chongh od-KHO-dzhee zah ——
MEE-noot.*

TICKETS
BILETY

156. Where is the ticket office?
Gdzie jest kasa biletowa?
gdzheh yest KAH-sah bee-leh-TOH-vah?

157. How much is a ticket to ——?
Ile kosztuje bilet do ——?
EE-leh kosh-TOO-yeh BEE-let doh ——?

158. (One-way, round trip) ticket.
(w jedną stronę, powrotny) bilet.
(*v YED-nohn STROH-neh, pov-ROT-nih*)
BEE-let.

159. (First, second, third) class.
(Pierwsza, druga, trzecia) klasa.
(*PYERV-shah, DROO-gah, TSHE-chah*)
KLAH-sah.

160. Can I go by way of ——?
Czy mogę pojechać przez ——?
chih MO-geh poh-YEH-hahch pshez ——?

161. How long is this ticket good?
Jak długo bilet jest ważny?
yahk DWOO-goh BEE-let yest VAZH-nih?

162. Can I get something to eat on the way?
Można dostać coś do jedzenia po drodze?
MOHZH-nah DOHS-tahch tsosh doh yeh-DZEH-nyah poh DROH-dzeh?

163. How much baggage may I take?
Ile bagażu mogę zabrać?
EE-leh bah-GAH-zhoo MOH-geh ZAH-brach?

164. How much per kilogram for excess?
Ile kosztuje dodatkowy kilogram?
EE-leh kosh-TOO-yeh doh-daht-KOH-vih kee-LO-grahm?

165. Is there travel insurance?
Czy mogę dostać ubezpieczenie?
chih MOH-geh DOS-tach oo-bez-pyeh-CHEH-nyeh?

BAGGAGE
BAGAŻ

168. Where is the baggage checked?
Gdzie jest przechowalnia?
gdzheh yest psheh-kho-VAL-nyah?

169. I want to leave these bags for a while.
Chcę zostawić walizki na chwilę.
h-tseh zos-TAH-vich vah-LEES-kee nah KHVEE-leh.

170. Do I pay now or later?
Czy mam zapłacić teraz czy później?
chih mahm zah-PWAH-chich TE-rahz chih POOZH-nyay?

171. I want to take out my baggage.
Chcę odebrać mój bagaż.
h-TSEH oh-DEB-rach MOO-ee BAH-gahzh.

172. That is mine there.
Mój jest tam.
MOO-ee yest tahm.

173. Handle this very carefully.

Bardzo ostrożnie, proszę.

BAHR-dzo ost-ROZH-nyeh, PROH-sheh.

TRAIN AND CONDUCTOR
POCIĄG I KONDUKTOR

175. I am going by train to ——.

Jadę pociągiem do ——.

YAH-deh po-CHOHNG-yem doh ——.

176. Is the train for —— on time?

Czy pociąg do —— przyjdzie punktual-
nie?

*chih PO-chohng doh —— pshih-YEE-dzheh
poonk-too-AHL-nyeh?*

177. It is late.

Jest opóźniony.

yest oh-poozh-NYOH-nih.

178. At what platform is the train for ——?

Na którym peronie stoi pociąg do ——?

*nah KTOO-rim peh-ROH-nyeh STOH-ee
PO-chohng doh ——?*

179. Please (open, close) the window.

Proszę (otworzyć, zamknąć) okno.

*PROH-sheh (oht-VOH-zhich, ZAMK-
nohnch) OHK-noh.*

180. Where is the diner?

Gdzie jest wagon restauracyjny?

gdzneh yest VAH-gohn rest-ow-rah-TSIY-nih?

181. Can you give me a match?
 (*to M.*) Czy ma pan zapałkę?
 chih mah pahn zah-PAHW-keh?

182. What time is (breakfast, lunch, dinner)?
 O której godzinie jest (śniadanie, obiad, kolacja)?
 oh KTOO-ray go-DZHEE-nyeh yest (shnyah-DAH-nyeh, OH-byahd, koh-LAH-tsyah)?

AIRPLANE
SAMOLOT

185. Is there motor service to the airport?
 Czy autobusy jadą na lotnisko?
 chih ow-toh-BOO-sih YAH-dohn nah lot-NEES-koh?

186. At what time will they come for me?
 Kiedy przyjadą po mnie?
 KYEH-dih pshih-YAH-dohn poh mn-YEH?

187. When is there a plane to ——?
 Kiedy odlatuje samolot do ——?
 KYEH-dih ohd-lah-TOO-yeh sah-MO-lot doh ——?

188. Is food served on the plane?
 Czy jedzenie podają w samolocie?
 chih yeh-DZEH-nyeh poh-DAH-yohn v sah-mo-LO-cheh?

189. How many kilos may I take?
 Ile kilogramów mogę zabrać?
 EE-leh kee-loh-GRAH-moov MOH-geh ZAH-brach?

BUS
AUTOBUS

192. How often do busses go to ——?

> Jak często autobusy odjeżdżają do ——?
>
> *yahk CHENS-toh ow-toh-BOO-sih ohd-yezh-DZHAH-yoh doh ——?*

193. Can I buy an excursion ticket?

> Czy mogę kupić bilet wycieczkowy?
>
> *chih MOH-geh KOO-peech BEE-let vih-chech-KOH-vih?*

194. Is there a stop for lunch?

> Czy zatrzymują się na obiad?
>
> *chih zah-tshih-MOO-yohn sheh nah OHB-yahd?*

195. Can I stop overnight on the way?

> Czy mogę zatrzymać się na noc po drodze?
>
> *chih MOH-geh zah-TSHIH-mahch sheh nah nohts poh DROH-dzeh?*

BOAT
OKRĘT

198. Can I go by boat to ——?

> Czy mogę pojechać okrętem do ——?
>
> *chih MOH-geh poh-YEH-hahch ohk-REN-tem doh ——?*

199. When does the next boat leave?

> Kiedy odjeżdża następny okręt?
>
> *KYEH-dih ohd-YEZH-dzah · nahs-TEMP-nih OHK-rent?*

200. When must I go on board?
Kiedy muszę być na okręcie?
KYEH-dih MOO-sheh bich̄ nah ohk-REN-
chh?

201. Can I land at ——?
Czy mogę wylądować w ——?
chih MOH-geh vih-lohn-DOH-vahch̄ v ——?

202. Are meals served on board?
Czy posiłki są podawane na okręcie?
chih poh-SH̄EEL-kee sohn poh-dah-VAH-neh
nah ohk-REN̄-cheh?

203. The captain. The-bursar.
Kapitan. Kwestor.
kah-PEE-tahn. KVEH-stor.

204. The steward. The deck.
Stuart. Pokład.
STOO-ahrt. POH-kwahd.

205. I want to rent a deck chair.
Chcę wynająć krzesło na pokładzie.
h-TSEH vih-NAH-yohnch̄ KSHES-woh nah
poh-KWAH-dz̄heh.

206. I am seasick.
Mam chorobę morską.
mahm kho-ROH-beh MOR-skohn.

207. I am going to my cabin.
Idę do mojej kabiny.
EE-deh doh MOH-yay kah-BEE-nih.

208. Let's go to the (dining room, bar).

Chodźmy do (jadalni, baru).

HOD$\overline{ZH}$-mih doh (yah-DAHL-nee, BAH-roo).

209. A life boat.   A life preserver.

Łódź ratunkowa.   Koło ratunkowe.

woodż rah-toon-KOH-vah.   KOH-woh rah-toon-KOH-veh.

AUTOMOBILE
SAMOCHÓD

212. Where is a (gas station, garage)?

Gdzie jest (stacja benzynowa, stacja obsługi)?

gdżeh yest (STAH-tsyah ben-zih-NOH-vah, STAH-tsyah ob-SWOO-gee)?

213. Is the road good?

Czy ta droga jest dobra?

chih tah DROH-gah yest DOH-brah?

214. Can you recommend a mechanic?

Proszę polecić mechanika?

PROH-sheh poh-LEH-cheech meh-hah-NEE-kah?

215. Is it hard or dirt surface?

Czy to jest asfaltowa czy polna droga?

chih toh yest ahs-fahl-TOH-vah chih POHL-nah DROH-gah?

216. What town is this?

Co to za miasto?

tsoh toh zah MYAH-stoh?

217. Where does that road go?

Dokąd prowadzi ta droga?

DOH-kohnd proh-VAH-dzhee tah DROH-gah?

218. I have an international driver's license.

Mam międzynarodowe prawo jazdy.

mahm myen-dzih-nah-roh-DOH-veh PRAH-voh YAHZ-dih.

219. How much is gas a liter?

Ile kosztuje litr benzyny?

EE-leh kohsh-TOO-yeh LEEtr behn-ZIH-nih?

220. Give me —— liters.

Proszę mi dać —— litrów.

PRO-sheh mee dahch —— LEET-roov.

221. Please change the oil.

Proszę zmienić oliwę.

PROH-sheh ZMYEH-neech oh-LEE-veh.

222. (Light, medium, heavy) oil.

(Lekka, średnia, ciężka) oliwa.

(LEHK-kah, SHRED-nyah, CHEHZH-kah) oh-LEE-vah.

223. Put water in the battery.

Proszę wlać wodę do akumulatora.

PROH-sheh vlahch VOH-deh doh ah-koo-moo-lah-TOH-rah.

224. Will you lubricate the car?

Proszę naoliwić auto?

PROH-sheh nah-oh-LEE-veech OW-toh?

225. Could you wash it?
  (*to M.*) Czy może pan wymyć auto?
  chih MO-zheh pahn VIH-mich OW-toh?

226. Tighten the brakes.
  Przykręcić hamulce.
  pshih-KREN-cheech ha-MOOL-tseh.

227. Will you check the tires?
  Proszę sprawdzić opony?
  PROH-sheh SPRAHV-dzheech oh-POH-nih?

228. Can you fix the flat tire?
  (*to M.*) Czy może pan naprawić oponę?
  *chih MOH-zhe pahn nah-PRAH-veech oh-
  POH-neh?*

229. A puncture.
  Dziura.
  DZHOO-rah.

230. The —— does not work well.
  —— nie pracuje dobrze.
  —— nyeh prah-TSOO-yeh DOHB-zheh.

231. What is wrong?
  Co się stało?
  tsoh sheh STAH-woh?

232. There is a (grinding, leak, noise).
  Tam jest (zgrzyt, wyciek, hałas).
  tahm yest (zg-ZHIT, VIH-chek, HA-wahs).

233. The engine overheats.
  Motor przegrzewa się za szybko.
  *MOH-tohr psheh-GZHEH-vah sheh zah
  SHIB-koh.*

234. May I park here for a while?

Czy mogę ústawić tu auto na chwile?

chih MOH-geh oo-STAH-veech too OW-toh nah HVEE-leh?

235. The engine stalls.

Motor gaśnie.

MOH-tor GAHSH-nyeh.

236. I want to garage my car for the night.

Chcę postawić auto na noc do garażu.

h-tseh poh-STAH-veech OW-toh nah nohts doh gah-RAH-zhoo.

237. When does it (open, close)?

Kiedy się (otwiera, zamyka)?

KYEH-dih sheh (oht-VYEH-rah, zah-MIH-kah)?

PARTS OF THE CAR
CZĘŚCI AUTA

240. Accelerator.   Battery.

Pedał benzynowy.   Bateria.

PEH-dahll ben-zih-NOH-vih.   bah-TEHR-yah.

241. Bolt.   Brake.   Engine.

Swożeń   Hamulec.   Motor.

SVOH-zhen. ha-MOO-lets.   MOH-tohr.

242. Nut.   Spring.   Starter.

Muterka.   Sprężyna.   Starter.

moo-TEHR-kah.   spren-ZHI-nah.   STAHR-tehr.

243. Steering wheel. Head light.
Kierownica. Przednie światła.
*kyeh-rohv-NEE-tsah.   PSHED-nyeh
SHVYAT-wah.*

244. Tail light. Tube. Tire.
Tylne światła. Dętka. Opona.
*TILL-neh SHVYAHT-wah. DENT-kah.
oh-POH-nah.*

245. Spare tire.
Opona zapasowa.
oh-POH-nah zah-pah-SOH-vah.

246. Wheel (front, back, left, right).
Koło (przednie, tylne, lewe, prawe).
*KOH-woh (PSHED-nyeh, TILL-neh, LEH-
veh, PRAH-veh).*

TOOLS AND EQUIPMENT
NARZEDZIA I EKWIPUNEK

248. Chains. Hammer. Jack.
Łańcuchy. Młot. Podnośnik.
*WAHN-tsoo-khih.   mwoht.   pohd-NOH-
shneek.*

249. Key. Pliers. Rope.
Klucz. Obcęgi. Sznur.
klooch. ohb-TSEN-ghee. schnoor.

250. Screwdriver. Tire pump. Wrench.
Śrubokręt. Pompa. Klucz francuski.
*shroo-BOH-krent. POHM-pah.   klooch
frahn-TSOOS-kee.*

HELP ON THE ROAD
POMOC W DRODZE

253. I am sorry to trouble you.
Przepraszam.
psheh-PRAH-shahm.

254. My car has broken down.
Moje auto się zepsuło.
MOH-yeh OW-tow sheh zep-SOO-woh.

255. Can you (tow, push) my car?
(*to M.*) Czy pan może (podciągnąć, popchnąć) moje auto?
chih pahn MOH-zheh (pohd-CHOHN-gnonch, POHP-hnonch) MOH-yeh OW-toh?

256. Can you help me jack up the car?
(*to M.*) Czy pan może pomóc mi założyć dźwig pod autem?
chih pahn MOH-zheh POH-moots mee zah-WOH-zhich dzh-VEEG pohd OW-tem?

257. Will you help me put on the spare?
(*to M.*) Czy może mi pan pomóc założyć oponę zapasową?
chih MOH-zheh mee pahn PO-moots zah-WOH-zhich oh-POH-neh zah-pah-SOH-voh?

258. Could you give me some gas?
(*to M.*) Czy może mi pan dać trochę benzyny?
chih MOH-zhee mee pahn dahch TRO-heh ben-ZIH-nih?

259. Will you take me to a garage?

Proszę mnie zaprowadzić do garażu?

PROH-sheh mnyeh zah-proh-VAH-dzheech doh gah-RAH-zhoo?

260. My car is stuck (in the mud).

Moje auto utkwiło (w błocie).

MOH-yeh OW-toh oot-KVEE-woh (v BWOH-cheh).

261. It is in the ditch.

Jest w rowie.

yest v ROH-vyeh.

ROAD SIGNS
NAPISY PRZYDROŻNE

264. Go.   265. Stop.   266. Steep grade.

Jedź!   Stój!   Ostre podgórze.

yehdzh.   STOO-ee.   OHST-reh pohd-GOO-zeh.

267. Boulevard.   268. High tension lines.

Bulwar.   Linie wysokiego napięcia.

BOOL-vahr.   LEEN-yeh vih-soh-KYEH-goh nah-PYEN-chah.

269. Narrow road.   270. Road repairs.

Wąska droga.   Naprawa drogi.

VON-skah DROH-gah.   nah-PRAH-vah DROH-gee.

271. Detour.   272. Intersection.

Objazd.   Skrzyżowanie.

OHB-yazd.   sk-shih-zhoh-VAH-nyeh.

273. Winding road.   274. Closed.
Serpentyna.   Zamknięte.
sehr-pen-TIH-nah.   zahm-KNYEN-teh.

275. Dip.   276. Keep right.   277. Sharp turn.
W dół.   Na prawo.   Ostry skręt.
v dooll.   nah PRAH-voh. OHS-trih ZAH- krent.

278. Curve.
Zakręt.
ZAH-krent.

279. Entrance.   280. Exit.   281. School.
Wjazd.   Wyjazd.   Szkoła.
vyahzd.   VIH-yahzd.   SHKOH-wah.

282. Parking.   283. No parking.   284. RR Crossing.
Postój Aut.   Postój aut wzbroniony.
Przejazd kolejowy.
POH-stooy owt.   POH-stooy owt vz-broh-NYO-nih.   PSHEH-yahzd koh-leh-YOH-vih.

285. Use second gear.   286. Slow down.
Jedź na drugim biegu.   Zwolnić.
yedzh nah DROO-geem BYE-goo.   ZVOHL-neech.

287. No thoroughfare.
Niema przejazdu.
nyeh-mah psheh-YAHZ-doo.

288. Stop!   289. Look!   290. Listen!
Stój!   Patrz!   Słuchaj!
STOO-y!   pahtzh!   SWOO-hie!

291. Danger. 292. Drive carefully.
Niebezpieczeństwo. Jedź ostrożnie.
*nyeh-bez-pyeh-CHEN-stvoh. yedzh ohs-
TROZH-nyeh.*

293. No (right, left) turn.
Niema (prawego, lewego) skrętu.
*nyeh-mah (prah-VEH-goh, leh-VEH-goh)
SKRENT-oo.*

294. Keep out.
Niema przejścia.
nyeh-mah PSHAYSH-chah.

295. (Narrow, temporary) bridge.
(Wąski, tymczasowy) mąst.
(VOHN-skee, tim-chah-SOH-vih) mohst.

296. One way.
Droga jednokierunkowa.
DROH-gah yehd-noh-kyeh-roon-KOH-vah.

297. No smoking.
Palenie wzbronione.
pah-LE-nyeh vz-broh-NYOH-neh.

298. Men. 299. Ladies.
Panowie. Panie.
pah-NOH-vyeh. PAH-nyeh.

LOCAL BUS AND STREETCAR
MIEJSCOWY AUTOBUS I TRAMWAJ

302. The bus stop. 303. The driver.
Przystanek autobusowy. Kierowca.
*pshis-TAH-nek ow-toh-boo-SOH-vih. kyeh-
ROHV-tsah.*

304. What (bus, car) do I take to ——?

Jaki (autobus, tramwaj) mam wziąść do ——?

YAH-kee (ow-TOH-boos, TRAHM-vie) mahm v-ZHONSH-ch doh ——?

305. Where does the (bus, car) for —— stop?

Gdzie się (autobus, tramwaj) do —— zatrzymuje?

gdzheh sheh (ow-TOH-boos, TRAHM-vie) doh —— zah-tzhih-MOO-yeh?

306. Do you go near ——?

(*to M.*) Czy pan dojeżdża do ——?

chih pahn doh-YEZH-dzhah doh ——?

307. How much is the fare?

Ile kosztuje bilet?

EE-leh kosh-TOO-yeh BEE-let?

308. A transfer, please.

Proszę o przesiadkę.

PROH-sheh oh psheh-SHAHD-keh.

309. Off next stop.   Two more stops.

Następny przystanek. Jeszcze dwa przystanki.

nahs-TEMP-nih pshis-TAH-nek. JESH-cheh dvah pshis-TAHN-kee.

TAXI
TAKSÓWKA

312. Please call a taxi for me.

Proszę zawołać taksówkę.

PROH-sheh zah-VOH-wahćh tahk-SOOV-keh.

313. How far is it?

Jak daleko?

yahk dah-LEH-koh?

314. How much will it cost?

Ile to będzie kosztowało?

EE-leh toh BEN-dźheh kohsh-toh-VAH-woh?

315. That is too much.

To jest za dużo.

toh yehst zah DOO-zho.

316. What do you charge per (hour, kilometer)?

Jaka jest taryfa za (godzinę, kilometr)?

YAH-kah yehst tah-RIH-fah zah (goh-DZHEE-neh, kee-LOH-metr)?

317. I just wish to drive around.

Chcę się tylko przejechać.

h-TSEH sheh TIHL-koh psheh-YEH-hahćh.

318. Please drive more (slowly, carefully).

Proszę jechać (wolniej, ostrożniej).

PROH-sheh YEH-hahćh (VOHL-nyay, ohs-TROHZH-nyay).

319. Stop here.   320. Wait for me.

Proszę stanąć.   Proszę zaczekać na mnie.
*PROH-sheh   STAH-nohnch.   PROH-sheh
zah-CHEH-kahch nah mn-YEH.*

321. How much do I owe?

Ile się należy?
EE-leh sheh nah-LEH-zhih?

LODGING: THE HOTEL
MIESZKANIE: HOTEL

324. Which hotel is (good, inexpensive)?

Jaki hotel jest (dobry, niedrogi)?
*YAH-kee HOH-tel yest (DOH-brih, nyeh-
DROH-gee)?*

325. The best hotel.

Najlepszy hotel.
nie-LEP-shih HOH-tel.

326. Not too expensive.

Nie zbyt drogi.
nyeh zbit DROH-gee.

**327. I (do not) want to be in the center of
town.**

(Nie) chcę być w centrum miasta.
*(nyeh) h-TSEH bich v TSEN-troom
MYAHS-tah.*

328. I have a reservation for ——.

Mam zarezerwowany pokój ——.
mahm zah-reh-zer-voh-VAH-nih poh-KOO-ee

329. I want to make a reservation.

Proszę zarezerwować dla mnie.

*PROH-sheh   zah-reh-zehr-VOH-vahch   dlah
mn-YEH.*

330. I want a room with meals.

Proszę o pokój z utrzymaniem.

*PROH-sheh   oh   poh-KOO-ee   z   oot-shih-
MAH-nyehm.*

331. I want a (single, double) room.

Proszę o (pojedyńczy, podwójny) pokój.

*PROH-sheh   oh   (poh-yeh-DIHN-chih,   pohd-
VOO-ee-nih) poh-KOO-ee.*

332. A suite.   A bed.

Apartament.   Łóżko.

ah-pahr-TAH-ment.   WOOZH-koh.

333. With (bath, shower, twin beds).

Z (łazienką, prysznicem, dwoma łóżkami).

*z (wah-ZHEN-koh, prish-NEE-tsem, DVOH-
mah woozh-KAH-mee).*

334. With (a window, a balcony).

Z (oknem, balkonem).

z (OHK-nem, bahl-KOH-nem).

335. A (front, back) room.

Frontowy pokój.   Pokój w oficynie.

*front-OH-vih   poh-KOO-ee.   poh-KOO-ee   v
oh-fee-TSIH-nyeh.*

336. For —— days.   For tonight.

Na —— dni.   Na jedną noc.

nah —— dnee.   nah YED-noh nohts.

337. For —— persons.
Dla —— osób.
dlah —— OH-soob.

338. What is the rate per day?
Ile kosztuje jeden dzień?
EE-leh kohsh-TOO-yeh YEH-den dz̄hen?

339. A week. A month.
Tydzień. Miesiąc.
TIH-dz̄hen. MYEH-shohnts.

340. On what floor?
Na którym piętrze?
nah KTOO-rim PYEN-tshe?

341. Upstairs. Downstairs.
Na górze. Na dole.
nah GOO-zheh. nah DOH-leh.

342. Is there an elevator?
Czy tam jest winda?
chih tahm yest VEEN-dah?

343. Running water. Hot water.
Bieżąca woda. Ciepła woda.
bye-ZHON-tsah VOH-dah. CHEP-wah VOH-dah.

344. I want a room higher up.
Proszę o pokój na wyższym piętrze.
PROH-sheh oh poh-KOO-ee nah VIZH-shim PYEN-tsheh.

345. On a lower floor.
Na niższym piętrze.
nah NIZH-shim PYEN-tsheh.

346. I should like to see the room.
Czy mogę obejrzeć ten pokój?
chih MOH-geh ob-AY-zhech ten poh-KOO-ee?

347. Where is the (bathroom, dining room)?
Gdzie jest (łazienka, jadalnia)?
gdzheh yest (wah-ZHEN-kah, yah-DAHL-nyah)?

348. I (do not) like this one.
Ten pokój mnie się (nie) podoba.
ten poh-KOO-ee mn-YEH sheh (nyeh) poh-DOH-bah.

349. Have you something better?
(*to M.*) Czy ma pan lepszy pokój?
chih mah pahn LEP-shih poh-KOO-ee?

350. Cheaper. Larger. Smaller.
Tańszy. Większy. Mniejszy.
TAHN-shih. VYENK-shih. mn-YAY-shih.

351. With more light. More air.
Więcej światła. Więcej powietrza.
VYEN-tsay sh-VYAHT-wah. VYEN-tsay poh-VYET-shah.

352. I have baggage at the station.
Mam bagaż na stacji.
mahm BAH-gahzh nah STAH-tsee.

353. Will you send for my bags?
(*to M.*) Czy może pan posłać po mój bagaż?
chih MOH-zheh pahn POHS-wach poh MOO-ee BAH-gahzh?

354. Here is the check for my trunk.
Tu jest kwit na mój kufer.
too yest kveet nah MOO-ee KOO-fer.

355. Please send —— to my room.
Proszę posłać —— do mojego pokoju.
PROH-sheh POHS-wahch —— doh moh-
YEH-goh poh-KOH-yoo.

356. Ice. Ice Water.
Lód. Woda z lodem.
Lood. VOH-dah z LOH-dem.

357. Please call me at —— o'clock.
Proszę zadzwonić do mnie o —— godzinie.
PROH-sheh zah-DZVOH-neech doh mn-
YEH oh —— goh-DZHEE-nyeh.

358. I want breakfast in my room.
Proszę o śniadanie w moim pokoju.
PROH-sheh oh sh-nyah-DAHN-yeh v MOH-
eem poh-KOH-yoo.

359. Could I have some laundry done?
Chciałbym oddać bieliznę do prania?
h-CHAHW-bim OD-dahch byeh-LEEZ-neh
doh PRAH-nyah?

360. I want some things pressed.
Chciałbym oddać niektóre rzeczy do
wyprasowania.
h-CHAHW-bim OD-dahch nyeh-KTOO-reh
ZHE-chih doh vih-prah-so-VAH-nyah.

361. My room key, please.
Proszę, o klucz do mojego pokoju.
PROH-sheh oh klooch doh moh-YEH-go poh-KOH-yoo.

362. Have I any letters, messages?
Czy ma pan dla mnie listy, polecenia?
chih mah pahn dlah mn-YEH LEES-tih, poh-leh-TSEH-nyah?

363. When does the mail come in?
Kiedy przychodzi poczta?
KYEH-dih p-shih-KHOHD-dz͞hee POHCH-tah?

364. What is my room number?
Jaki jest numer mojego pokoju?
YAH-kee yest NOO-mehr moh-YEH-goh poh-KOH-yoo?

365. I am leaving at ——.
Wychodzę o ——.
vih-KHOH-dzeh oh ——.

366. Please make out my bill.
Proszę o rachunek.
PROH-sheh oh rah-HOO-nek.

367. May I store baggage here until ——?
Czy mogę zostawić tutaj mój bagaż do
——?
chih MOH-geh zohs-TAH-veech TOO-tie MOO-ee BAH-gahzh doh ——?

CHAMBERMAID
POKOJOWA

368. Please (open, close) the windows.
Proszę (otworzyć, zamknąć) okna.
PROH-sheh (oht-VOH-zhĭch, ZAHMK-nohnch) OHK-nah.

369. Do not disturb me until ——.
Proszę nie przeszkadzać mi do ——.
PROH-sheh nyeh psheh-SHKAH-dzahch mee doh ——.

370. Please change the sheets today.
Proszę zmienić dzisiaj powleczenie.
PROH-sheh ZMYEH-neech DZHEE-shie pohv-leh-CHEH-nyeh.

371. Bring me another (blanket, pillow).
Proszę mi przynieść jeszcze jedną (kołdrę, poduszkę).
PROH-sheh mee PSHIH-nyesh-ch YEHSH-cheh YEHD-noh (KOW-dreh, poh-DOOSH-keh).

372. A pillow case.
Poszewka.
poh-SHEV-kah.

373. Hangers. 374. A glass. 375. The door.
Wieszak. Szklanka. Drzwi.
VYEH-shahk. sh-KLAHN-kah. dzh-VEE.

376. Soap. 377. Towels. 378. A candle.
Mydło. Ręczniki. Świeca.
MID-woh. rench-NEE-kee. SHVYEH-tsah.

379. The bathtub.   380. The sink.

Wanna.   Umywalnia.

VAHN-nah.   oo-mih-VAHL-nyah.

381. Drinking water.   382. Toilet paper.

Woda do picia.   Papier toaletowy.

*VOH-dah doh PEE-chah.   PAH-pyehr toh-
ah-leh-TOH-vih.*

See also COMMON OBJECTS, page 108

383. Is there always hot water?

Czy zawsze jest gorąca woda?

*chih ZAHV-sheh yest goh-ROHN-tsah VOH-
dah?*

APARTMENT
MIESZKANIE

385. I want a furnished apartment.

Chciałbym umeblowane mieszkanie.

*H-chahw-bim   oo-meb-loh-VAH-neh   myesh-
KAH-nyeh.*

386. —— bedrooms.

—— sypialnie.

—— sih-PYAHL-nyeh.

387. A dining room.   388. A kitchen.

Pokój stołowy.   Kuchnia.

*poh-KOO-ee   stoh-WOH-vih.   KOOKH-
nyah.*

389. A balcony.   390. A bathroom.

Balkon.   Łazienka.

BAHL-kon.   wah-ZHYEN-kah.

391. Is the linen furnished?
Czy otrzymam bieliznę pościelową?
chih oht-SHIH-mahm byeh-LEEZ-neh pohsh-cheh-LOH-voh?

392. How much is it a month?
Ile kosztuje miesięcznie?
EE-leh kosh-TOO-yeh myeh-SHENCH-nyeh?

393. Comforters. 394. Cutlery.
    395. Dishes.
Kołdry. Nakrycie stołowe. Naczynia.
KOW-drih. nahk-RIH-cheh stoh-WOH-veh. nah-CHIH-nyah.

396. Can I get a maid?
Czy mogę dostać służącą?
chih MOH-geh DOHS-tahch swoo-ZHON-tsoh?

397. Do you know a good cook?
(*to M.*) Czy pan może polecić dobrą
    kucharkę? (*F.*)
chih pahn MOH-zhe po-LEH-cheech DOHB-roh koo-KHAR-keh?

398. Where can I rent a garage?
Gdzię mogę wynająć garaż?
g-DZHEH MOH-geh vih-NAH-yohnch GAH-rahzh?

RESTAURANT AND FOOD
RESTAURACJA I ŻYWNOŚĆ

400. Where is there a good restaurant?
Gdzie tu jest dobra restauracja?
g-DZHEH too yest DOHB-rah res-tow-RAH-tsyah?

401. Breakfast. Lunch. Dinner.
Śniadanie. Obiad. Kolacja.
sh-nyah-DAH-nyeh. OHB-yahd. koh-LAH-tsyah.

402. Supper. A sandwich.
Kolacja. Kanapka.
koh-LAH-tsyah. kah-NAHP-kah.

403. Between what hours is dinner served?
O której godzinie podają kolację?
oh KTOO-ray go-DZHEE-nyeh poh-DAH-yoh koh-LAH-tsyeh?

404. Can we (lunch, dine) now?
Czy możemy dostać teraz (obiad, kolację)?
chih moh-ZHEH-mih DOHS-tahch TEH-rahz (OHB-yahd, koh-LAH-tsyeh)?

405. The waitress. The waiter.
Kelnerka. Kelner.
kel-NER-kah. KEL-ner.

406. Give me a table near the window.
Proszę o stolik koło okna.
PROH-sheh oh STOH-leek KOH-woh OHK-nah.

407. At the side. In the corner.
Z boku. W kącie.
z BOH-koo. v KON-cheh.

408. Is this table reserved?
Czy ten stolik jest zarezerwowany?
chih ten STO-leek yest zah-reh-zer-voh-VAH-nih?

409. That table will be free soon.
Tamten stolik zwolni się wkrótce.
TAHM-ten STOH-leek ZVOHL-nee sheh VKROOT-tseh.

410. We want to dine à la carte.
Chcemy zamówić à la carte.
h-TSEH-mih zah-MOO-vich a la cart.

411. Please serve us quickly.
Proszę podać nam szybko.
PROH-sheh POH-dahch nahm SHIB-koh.

412. Bring me the (menu, wine list).
Proszę mi podać (menu, spis win).
PROH-sheh mee POH-dahch (MEN-u, spees veen).

413. I want something (simple, not too spicy).
Proszę o coś (zwykłego, nie ostrego).
PROH-sheh oh tsosh (zvih-KWEH-goh, nyeh OHST-rego).

414. A napkin. 415. A glass.
Serwetka. Szklanka.
ser-VET-kah. SHKLAHN-kah.

416. A plate. 417. A knife.
Talerz. Nóż.
TAH-lezh. noozh.

418. A fork. 419. A large spoon.
Widelec. Łyżka stołowa.
vee-DEH-lets. WIZH-kah stoh-WOH-vah.

420. A teaspoon. 421. The bread.
Łyżeczka. Chleb.
wih-ZHECH-kah. hleb.

422. The butter. 423. The cream.
Masło. Śmietanka.
MAHS-woh. shmyeh-TAHN-kah.

424. The sugar. 425. The salt. 426. The pepper.
Cukier. Sól. Pieprz.
TSOO-kyehr. sool. PYEHP-sh.

427. The sauce. 428. The oil. 429. The vinegar.
Sos. Oliwa. Ocet.
sohs. oh-LEE-vah. OH-tset.

430. This is not clean.
To nie jest czyste.
toh nyeh yest CHIS-teh.

431. (A little) more of this.
(Trochę) więcej tego.
(TROH-kheh) VYEN-tsay TEH-goh.

432. I have had enough, thanks.
Mam dosyć, dziękuję.
mahm DOH-sich, dzhen-KOO-yeh.

433. I like the meat (rare, well done).
Lubię mięso (średnio, dobrze wysmażone).
LOO-byeh   MYEN-soh   (SHRED-nyoh,
DOHB-zhéh   vis-mah-ZHO-neh).

434. This is (undercooked, overcooked).
To jest (niedogotowane, przegotowane).
toh yest   (nyeh-doh-goh-toh-VAH-neh, psheh-
goh-toh-VAH-neh).

435. This is too (tough, sweet, sour).
To jest za (twarde, słodkie, kwaśne).
toh yest zah   (TVAHR-deh, SWOHD-kyeh,
KVAHSH-neh).

436. This is cold.
To jest zimne.
toh yest ZHEEM-neh.

437. Take it away.
Proszę to zabrać.
PROH-sheh toh ZAHB-rahch.

438. I did not order this.
(*M.*) Nie zamawiałem tego.
nyeh zah-mah-VYAH-wehm TEH-goh.

439. May I change this for ——?
Czy mogę to zamienić na ——?
chih MOH-geh toh zah-MYEH-neech nah
——?

440. Ask the head-waiter to come here.
Proszę poprosić kierownika.
PROH-sheh poh-PROH-sheech   kyeh-rohv-
NEE-kah.

441. The check, please.
Proszę o rachunek.
PROH-sheh oh rah-HOO-nehk.

442. Kindly pay at the cashier's.
Proszę zapłacić kasjerowi.
PROH-sheh zahp-WAH-cheech kahs-yehr-OH-vee.

443. Is the tip included?
Czy napiwek jest włączony?
chih nah-PEE-vek yest vwohn-CHOH-nih?

444. Keep the change.
Proszę zatrzymać resztę.
PROH-sheh zah-TSHIH-mahch RESH-teh.

445. There is a mistake in the bill.
W rachunku jest błąd.
v rah-HOON-koo yest bwohnd.

446. What are these charges for?
Za co są te pozycje w rachunku?
zah tsoh sohn teh poh-ZIT-syeh v rah-HOON-koo?

CAFE
KAWIARNIA

448. Bartender.   449. A cocktail.
Barman.   Cocktail.
BAHR-mahn.   KOK-tail.

450. A (an alcoholic) drink.
Napój (wyskokowy).
nah-POO-ee (vis-koh-KOH-vih).

451. A fruit drink.   452. A liqueur.
Napój owocowy.   Likier.
nah-POO-ee oh-voh-TSOH-vih.   LEE-kyehr.

453. A (small, large) bottle of ——.
(Mała, duża) butelka ——.
(MAH-wah, DOO-zhah) boo-TEL-kah ——.

454. A glass of ——.
Szklanka.
SHKLAHN-kah ——.

455. Beer (Light, dark).
Piwo (jasne, ciemne).
PEE-voh (YAHS-neh, CHEM-neh).

456. Wine (red, white).
Wino (czerwone, białe).
VEE-noh (cher-VOH-neh, BYAH-weh).

457. Whiskey (and soda).
Whiskey (i woda sodowa).
WIS-kee (ee VOH-dah soh-DOH-vah).

458. Brandy.
Koniak.
KOH-nyahk.

459. Let's have ,another.
Jeszcze jeden.
YESH-cheh YEH-den.

FOOD
ŻYWNOŚĆ

461. Soup (chicken, vegetable).
Zupa (rosół, jarzynowa).
ZOO-pah (ROH-sool, yah-zhih-NOH-vah).

462. Eggs (scrambled, fried).
>   Jajka (jajecznica, sadzone).
>   *YAHY-kah (yah-yech-NEE-tsa, sah-DZOH-neh).*

463. Eggs (Soft-boiled, hard-boiled).
>   Jajka na miękko, jajka na twardo.
>   *YAHY-kah nah MYEN-koh, YAHY-kah nah TVAHR-doh.*

464. Omelette.
>   Omlet.
>   *OHM-let.*

ENTREE: MEATS AND FISH
MIĘSO I RYBY.

467. Roast beef.
>   Pieczeń wołowa.
>   *PYEH-chehn̄ voh-WOH-vah.*

468. Carp.   469. Chicken (fried).
>   Karp. .Kura (smażona).
>   *kahrp. KOO-rah (smah-ZHOH-nah).*

470. Duck.   471. Goose.   472. Lamb.
>   Kaczka. Gęś. Baranina.
>   *KAHCH-kah. gensh̄. bah-rah-NEE-nah.*

473. Liver.   474. Lobster.   475. Pork.
>   Wątróbka. Homar. Wieprzowina.
>   *von-TROOB-kah. HOH-mar. vyep-shoh-VEE-nah.*

476. Steak.
>   Befsztyk.
>   *BEF-shtik.*

477. Slice of ——.
Kawałek ——.
kah-VAH-wek ——.

478. Sardine.   479. Salmon.
Sardynka.   Łosoś.
sahr-DIN-kah.   WOH-sosh.

480. Sausage.   481. Veal.
Kiełbasa.   Cielęcina.
kyel-BAH-sah.   cheh-len-CHEE-nah.

VEGETABLES AND SALAD
JARZYNY I SALATY

**482. Asparagus.   483. Beans.
      484. Cabbage.**
Szparagi.   Fasola.   Kapusta.
*shpah-RAH-gee.   fah-SOL-ah.   kah-POOS-
tah.*

485. Cauliflower.
Kalafior.
kah-LAH-fyor.

486. Carrots.   487. Corn.   488. Cucumber.
Marchewka.   Kukurydza.   Ogórek.
*mar-HEV-ka.   koo-koo-RIH-dzah.   oh-GOO-
rek.*

**489. Garlic.   490. Lettuce.   491. Mush-
rooms.**
Czosnek.   Sałata.   Grzyby.
*CHOHS-nek.   sah-WAH-tah.   g-ZHIH-
bih.*

492. Onion.   493. Peas.   494. Pepper.
Cebula.   Groszek zielony.   Pieprz.
tseh-BOO-lah.   GRO-shek   z̄heh-LOH-nih.
PYEHP-sh.

495. Potatoes (fried, boiled, mashed).
Ziemniaki (smażone, gotowane, pure).
z̄hem-NYAH-kee (smah-Z̄HOH-neh, goh-toh-
VAH-neh, POOH-reh).

496. Radishes.   497. Spinach.
498. Tomatoes.
Rzodkiewka.   Szpinak.   Pomidory.
zhohd-KYEV-kah.   SHPEE-nahk.   poh-
mee-DOH-rih.

FRUITS
OWOCE

500. Apple.   501. Apple sauce.
Jabłko.   Kompot z jabłek.
YAHB-koh.   KOHM-poht z YAHB-wek.

502. Grapes.   503. Grapefruit.
Winogrona.   Grejpfrut.
vee-noh-GROH-nah.   GRAYP-froot.

504. Lemon.   505. Melon.   506. Water-
melon.
Cytryna.   Melon.   Arbuz.
tsit-RIH-nah.   MEH-lohn.   AHR-booz.

507. Nuts.
Orzechy.
oh-Z̄HEH-hih.

508. Olives (ripe, green).
Oliwki (dojrzałe, zielone).
oh-LEEV-kee (doh-y-ZHAH-weh, zheh-LOH-neh).

509. Orange. 510. Peach.
Pomarańcza. Brzoskwinia.
poh-mah-RAHN-chah. b-zhosk-VEE-nyah.

511. Raisins. 512. Raspberries.
Rodzynki. Maliny.
roh-DZIN-kee. mah-LEE-nih.

513. Strawberries. 514. Cherries.
Truskawki. Wiśnie.
troos-KAHV-kee. VEESH-nyeh.

BEVERAGES
NAPOJE

517. Coffee (black, with cream).
Kawa (czarna, ze śmietanką).
KAH-vah (CHAR-nah, zeh sh-myeh-TAHN-kohn).

518. Lemonade. 519. Milk.
Lemoniada. Mleko.
leh-moh-NYAH-dah. MLEH-koh.

520. Tea (with lemon, with milk).
Herbata (z cytryną, z mlekiem).
her-BAH-tah (z tsit-RIH-noh, z MLEH-kyem).

DESSERTS
DESERY

522. Cake.   523. Cookies.
Ciasto.   Ciasteczka.
CHAHS-toh.   chahs-TECH-kah.

524. Chocolate.   525. Vanilla.
Czekolada.   Wanilia.
cheh-koh-LAH-dah.   vah-NEEL-yah.

526. Custard.   527. Ice-cream.
Budyń.   Lody.
BOO-dihn.   LOH-dih.

528. Jam.
Marmelada.
mahr-MEH-lah-dah.

OTHERS
INNE

530. Cheese.   531. Mustard.
Ser.   Musztarda.
sehr.   moosh-TAHR-dah.

532. Noodles.   533. Rice.
Makaron.   Ryż.
mah-KAH-ron.   rizh.

534. Oatmeal.   535. Toast.
Owsianka.   Grzanka.
ohv-SHAHN-kah.   GZHAHN-kah.

CHURCH
KOŚCIÓŁ

538. (Catholic, Anglican) Church.

(Katolicki, anglikański) kościół.

(*kah-toh-LEETS-kee,   ahn-glee-KAHN̄-skee*)
KOHSH̄-cho̅ol.

539. A Protestant Church.

Protestancki kościół.

proh-tes-TAHN-tskee KOHSH̄-cho̅ol.

540. A Synagogue.

Synagoga.

sih-nah-GOH-gah

541. Where is there a service in English?

Gdzie jest nabożeństwo w języku angiel-
skim?

*gdz̄heh yest nah-boh-ZHAYN̄ST-voh v yen-
ZIH-koo ahn-GYEL-skeem?*

542. When is the (service, mass)?

Kiedy jest (nabożeństwo, msza)?

*KYEH-dih yest (nah-boh-ZHAYN̄ST-voh,
mshah)?*

**543. Is there an English-speaking (priest,
rabbi, pastor)?**

Czy tam jest (ksiądz, rabin, pastor)
mówiący po angielsku?

*chih tahm yest (k-sho̅nts, RAH-been, PAHS-
tor) moo-VYOHN-tsih poh ahn-GYEL-
skoo?*

SIGHTSEEING
ZWIEDZANIE

545. I want a guide who speaks English.
Chcę przewodnika mówiącego po angielsku.
*h-TSEH psheh-vod-NEE-kah moo-vyohn-
TSEH-goh poh ahn-GYEL-skoo.*

546. What is the charge per (hour, day)?
Ile kosztuje na (godzinę, dzień)?
*EE-leh, kohsh-TOO-yeh nah (goh-D̄Z̄HEE-
neh, dz̄hen̄)?*

547. Native arts and crafts.
Sztuka krajowa i przemysł.
*SHTOO-kah krah-YOH-vah ee PSHEH-
mis-ll.*

548. Painting. 549. Sculpture.
Malarstwo. Rzeźba.
mah-LAHRS-tvoh. Z̄HEZ̄H-bah.

550. Shall I have time to visit the museums?
Czy będę miał czas na zwiedzenie muzeum?
*chih BEN-deh myahw chahs nah z-vyeh-
DZEH-nyeh moo-Z̄EH-oom?*

551. The cathedral. 552. The monastery.
Katedra. Klasztor.
kah-TED-rah. KLAHSH-tor.

553. The castle. 554. The temple.
Zamek. Świątynia.
Z̄AH-mek. S̄H̄VYOHN-tih-nyah.

555. Is it still open?
Czy jest jeszcze otwarte?
chih yest YESH-cheh oht-VAHR-teh?

556. How long does it stay open?
Jak długo będzie otwarte?
yahk DWOO-goh BEN-dzheh oht-VAHR-teh?

557. How long must I wait?
Jak długo muszę czekać?
yahk DWOO-goh MOO-sheh CHEH-kahch?

558. Where is the (entrance, exit)?
Gdzie jest (wejście, wyjście)?
G-dzheh yest (VAYSH-cheh, vih-EESH-cheh)?

559. What is the price of admission?
Ile kosztuje bilet?
EE-leh kosh-TOO-yeh BEE-let?

560. Do we need a guide?
Czy potrzebny przewodnik?
chih poht-sheh-bnih psheh-VOHD-neek?

561. How much is the guidebook?
Ile kosztuje przewodnik?
EE-leh kosh-TOO-yeh psheh-VOHD-neek?

562. May I take photographs?
Czy wolno fotografować?
chih VOHL-noh foh-toh-grah-FOH-vach?

563. Do you sell postcards?
(*to M.*) Czy pan sprzedaje widokówki?
chih pahn sp-shed-DAH-yeh vee-doh-KOOV-kee?

564. Do you have a book in English about ——?

(*to M.*) Czy pan ma książkę po angielsku o ——?

chih pahn mah KSHOHN-shkeh poh ahn-GYEL-skoo oh ——?

565. Take me back to the hotel.

Proszę mnie zaprowadzić spowrotem do hotelu.

PROH-sheh mn-YEH zah-proh-VAH-dzheech spov-ROH-tem doh hoh-TEH-loo.

566. Go back by way of ——.

Prosze iść spowrotem przez ——.

PROH-sheh EESH-ch spov-ROH-tem pshez ——.

AMUSEMENTS

Rozrywki.

568. A concert. 569. Movies. 570. Folk dances.

Koncert. Kino. Tańce ludowe.

KOHN-tsert. KEE-noh. TAHN-tseh loo-DOH-veh.

571. The beach. 572. Tennis. 573. Horse-racing.

Plaża. Tenis. Wyścigi konne.

PLAH-zhah. TEH-nees. vish-CHEE-gee KOHN-neh.

574. Skiing. 575. Skating. 576. Soccer.

Jazda na nartach. Jazda na łyżwach.
Piłka nozna.

*YAHZ-dah nah NAHR-tahkh. YAHZ-dah
nah WIZH-vahkh. PEEW-kah NOHZH-
nah.*

577. Night Club. 578. The opera. 579. The theatre.

Nocny lokal. Opera. Teatr.
*NOHTS-nih LOH-kal. oh-PEH-rah. TEH-
ahtr.*

580. Is there a matinee today?

Czy dzisiaj jest przedstawienie popołud-
niowe?

*chih dzhee-shie yest pshed-stah-VYEH-nyeh
poh-poh-WOOD-nyo-veh?*

581. Cover charge. 582. Minimum.

Minimum konsumcji. Minimum.
*mee-NEE-moom kohn-SOOM-tsee. mee-
NEE-moom.*

583. When does the performance start?

O której godzinie zaczyna się przedstawienie?

*oh KTOO-ray goh-DZHEE-nyeh zah-CHIH-
nah sheh pshed-stah-VYEH-nyeh?*

584. Where can we go to dance?

Dokąd możemy iść tańczyć?
*DOH-kohnd moh-ZHEM-mih EESH-ch
TAHN-chich?*

585. Have you any seats for tonight?

(*to M.*) Czy ma pan bilety na dziś wieczór?

chih mah pahn bee-LEH-tih nah dźheesh VYEH-choor?

586. What shall we wear?

Jak się mamy ubrać?

yahk sheh MAH-mih OOB-rahch?

587. A reserved seat.

Zarezerwowane miejsce.

zah-reh-zer-voh-VAH-neh MYAYS-tseh.

588. In the balcony. The box. The usher.

Balkon. Loża. Biletowy.

BAHL-kohn. LO-zhah. bee-leh-TOH-vih.

589. Can I (see, hear) well from there?

Czy będę dobrze (widział, słyszał) stamtąd?

chih BEN-deh DOHB-zheh (VEE-dźhah, SWIH-shahll) STAHM-tohnd?

590. Not too (near, far).

Nie za (daleko, blisko).

nyeh zah (dah-LEH-koh, BLEES-koh).

591. The music is excellent.

Doskonała muzyka.

doh-skoh-NAH-wah moo-ZIH-kah.

592. This is very (interesting, funny).

To jest bardzo (interesujące, śmieszne).

toh yest BAHRD-zoh (een-teh-reh-soo-YOHN-tseh, SHMYESH-neh).

593. May I have this dance?
Czy mogę prosić o ten taniec?
chih MOH-geh PROH-sheech oh tehn TAHN-nyets?

594. Is this the intermission?
Czy to jest przerwa?
chih toh yest PSHER-vah?

SHOPPING AND PERSONAL SERVICES
ZAPUKY I OBSŁUGA

596. I want to go shopping.
Chce iść po zakupy.
kh-TSEH EESH-ch poh zah-KOO-pih.

597. Where is the bakery?
Gdzie jest piekarnia?
g-DZHEH yest pyeh-KAHR-nyah?

598. A candy store. 599. A cigar store.
Sklep z czekoladą. Sklep tytoniowy.
sklep z cheh-koh-LAH-doh, sklep tih-toh-NYOH-vih.

600. A clotl.ing store. 601. A department store.
Sklep z ubraniami. Dom towarowy.
sklep z oob-rah-NYAH-mee. dohm toh-vah-ROH-vih.

602. A drug store. 603. A grocery.
Apteka. Sklep spożywczy.
ahp-TEH-kah. sklep spoh-ZHIV-chih.

604. A hardware store.   605. A hat shop.
Sklep towarów żelaznych. Sklep z kapeluszami.
sklep toh-VAH-roov zheh-LAHZ-nikh. sklep z kah-peh-loo-SHAH-mee.

606. A jewelry store.   607. A shoe store.
Sklep jubilerski. Sklep z obuwiem.
sklep yoo-bee-LER-skee. sklep z ohb-OO-vyem.

608. A meat market.   609. A tailor shop.
Rzeźnik. Krawiec.
ZHEH-zhneek. KRAH-vvets.

610. Shoemaker.   611. Watchmaker.
Szewc. Zegarmistrz.
shevts. zeh-GAHR-meest-ch.

See also CLOTHING, COMMON OBJECTS

614. Sale.   Bargain sale.
Sprzedaż. Wyprzedaż.
sp-SHEH-dahzh. vip-SHEH-dahzh.

615. I want to buy ——.
Chcę kupić ——.
h-TSEH KOO-peech ——.

616. I (do not) like this.
To mi się (nie) podoba.
toh mee sheh (nyeh) poh-DOH-bah.

617. How much is that?
Ile to kosztuje?
EE-leh toh kohsh-TOO-yeh?

618. It is very expensive.
To jest bardzo drogo.
toh yest BAHRD-zoh DROH-goh.

619. I prefer something (better, cheaper).
Wolę coś (lepszego, tańszego).
VOH-leh tsohsh (lep-SHEH-goh, tahn-SHEH-goh).

620. Show me some others.
Proszę pokazać coś innego.
PROH-sheh poh-KAH-zahch tsosh een-NEH-'goh.

621. May I try this on?
Czy mogę to przymierzyć?
chih MOH-geh toh pshih-MYEH-zhich?

6⒉. Can I order one?
Czy mogę zamówić jedno?
chih MOH-geh zah-MOO-veech YED-noh?

623. How long will it take?
Jak to długo potrwa?
yahk toh DWOO-goh POHTR-vah?

624. Please take my measurements.
Proszę wziąć moją miarę.
PROH-sheh v-ZHOHNSH-ch MOH-yoh. MYAH-reh.

See also MEASUREMENTS.

626. It does not fit me.
To nie pasuje na mnie.
toh nyeh pah-SOO-yeh nah mn-YEH.

627. It is (not) becoming to me.
W tym mi nie do twarzy.
v tihm mee nyeh doh TVAH-zhih.

628. Will you wrap this, please?
Proszę to zapakować.
PROH-sheh toh zah-pah-KOH-vahch.

629. Can you ship this to ——?
Czy może pan wysłać to do ——?
chih MOH-zheh pahn VIS-wahch toh doh
——?

POST OFFICE
POCZTA

632. Where is the post office?
Gdzie jest urząd pocztowy?
g-DZHEH yest OO-zhohnd pohch-TOH-vih?

633. A (postcard, letter) to ——.
(Karta pocztowa, list) do ——.
(KAHR-tah pohch-TOH-vah, leest) doh ——.

634. How many stamps do I need?
Ile mam nalepić znaczków pocztowych?
EE-leh mahm nah-LEH-peech ZNAHCH-
koov pohch-TOH-vikh?

635. There is nothing dutiable on this.
Na to niema cła.
nah toh NYEH-mah ts-WAH.

636. Will this go out today?
Czy to odejdzie dzisiaj?
chih toh oh-DAY-dzheh DZHEE-shie?

637. Give mc a receipt, please.

Proszę o pokwitowanie.

PROH-sheh oh pohk-vee-toh-VAH-nyeh.

638. I want to send a money order.

Chcę wysłać przekaz pieniężny.

h-TSEH VIS-wahch PSHEH-kahz pyeh-NYEN-zhnih.

639. To which window do I go?

Do którego okienka mam się udać?

doh ktoo-REH-goh oh-KYEHN-kah mahm sheh OO-dahch?

640. By airmail.   641. Parcel post.

Poczta lotnicza.   Poczta zwyczajna.

POHCH-tah loht-NEE-chah.   POHCH-tah zvih-CHIE-nah.

642. Registered.   643. Special Delivery.

List polecony.   Ekspres.

leest poh-leh-TSOH-nih.   EX-press.

BANK
BANK

646. Where is the nearest bank?

Gdzie jest najbliższy bank?

g-DZHEH yest nie-BLEEZH-shih bahnk?

647. At which window can I cash this?

Przy którym oknie mogę wymienić to?

pshih KTOO-rim OHK-nyeh MOH-gheh vih-MYEH-neech toh?

648. Can you change this for me?
   (*to M.*) Czy pan to może zmienić?
   chih pahn toh MOH-zheh ZMYEH-neech?

649. Will you cash a check?
   Czy moge otrzymać pieniądze za mój czek?
   *chih   MOH-geh   oht-SHIH-mahch   pyeh-
   NYOHN-dzeh zah MOO-ee chek?*

650. Do not give me large bills.
   Proszę mi nie dawać wysokich banknotów.
   *PROH-sheh mee (nyeh DAH-vahch vih-SOH-
   keekh bahnk-NOH-toov.*

651. May I have some change?
   Czy mogę otrzymać bilon?
   chih MOH-geh oht-SHIH-mahch BEE-lohn?

652. Letter of credit.
   Akredytywa.
   ahk-reh-dih-TIH-vah.

653. I have traveler's checks.
   Mam czeki bankowe.
   mahm CHEH-kee bahn-KOH-vch.

654. A bank draft.
   Trata bankowa.
   TRAH-tah bahn-KOH-vah.

**655. What is the exchange rate on the
    dollar?**
   Jaki jest kurs dolara?
   YAH-kee yest koors doh-LAH-rah?

BOOKSTORE AND STATIONER'S
KSIĘGARNIA I SKLEP MATERIAŁÓW PIŚMIENNYCH

658. Where is there a bookstore?
Gdzie jest księgarnia?
g-DZHEH yest kshen-GAHR-nyah?

659. A stationer's. 660. A newsstand.
Sklep materiałów piśmiennych. Kiosk z gazetami.
sklep mah-ter-yah-WOOV. peesh-myen-nikh. kyohsk z gah-zeh-TAH-mee.

**661. Newspapers. 662. Magazines.
663. Weeklies.**
Gazety. Czasopisma. Tygodniki.
gah-ZEH-tih. chah-soh-PEES-mah. tih-gohd-NEE-kee.

664. A dictionary. 665. A guidebook.
Słownik. Przewodnik.
SWOHV-neek. psheh-VOHD-neek.

666. A map of ——.
Mapa ——.
MAH-pah ——.

667. Postcards. 668. Playing cards.
Karty pocztowe. Karty do gry.
KAHR-tih pohch-TOH-veh. KAHR-tih doh grih.

669. Greeting cards.
Karty z powinszowaniami.
KAHR-tih z poh-veen-shoh-vah-NYAH-mee.

670. Writing paper.   671. Ink.   672. Blotter.
Papier do pisania.   Atrament.   Bibuła.
*PAH-pyer   doh   pee-SAH-nyah.   aht-RAH-
ment.   bee-BOO-wah.*

673. Envelopes (airmail).   674. A pencil.
Koperty (lotnicze).   Ołówek
*koh-PER-tih   (loht-NEE-cheh).   oh-WOO-
vek.*

675. A fountain pen.
Wieczne pióro.
VYECH-neh PYOO-roh.

676. (Strong) string.   677. An eraser.
(Mocny) sznurek.   Gumka.
(MOHTS-nih) SHNOOR-rek.   GOOM-kah.

**678. Typewriter ribbon.   679. Carbon
paper.**
Taśma do maszyny do pisania.   Kalka.
*TAH$\overline{SH}$-mah doh mah-SHIH-nih doh pee-
SAH-nyah.   KAHL-kah.*

680. Tissue paper.   681. Wrapping paper.
Bibułka.   Papier do pakowania.
*bee-BOOL-kah.   PAH-pyehr   doh   pah-koh-
VAH-nyah.*

CIGAR STORE
SKLEP TYTONIOWY

684. Where is the nearest cigar store?
Gdzie jest najbliższy sklep tytoniowy?
*g-D$\overline{Z}$HEH jest nie-BLEE$\overline{Z}$H-shih sklep tih-
t$_{v}$h-NYOH-vih?*

685. I want some cigars.
Proszę o cygara.
PROH-sheh oh tsih-GAH-rah.

686. A pack of cigarettes, please.
Proszę o paczkę papierosów.
PROH-sheh oh PAHCH-keh pah-pyeh-ROH-soov.

687. I need a lighter.
Proszę o zapalniczkę.
PROH-sheh oh zah-pahl-NEECH-keh.

688. Flint.   Fluid.
Kamień do zapalniczki.   Benzyna.
KAH-myehn doh zah-pahl-NEECH-kee.   ben-ZIH-nah.

689. Matches.   A pipe.
Zapałki.   Fajka.
zah-PAHL-kee.   FIE-kah.

690. Pipe tobacco.   A pouch.
Tytoń do fajki.   Woreczek na tytoń.
TIH-tohn doh FIE-kee.   voh-REH-chehk nah TIH-tohn.

BARBER SHOP AND BEAUTY PARLOR
ZAKLAD FRYZJERSKI I SALON KOSME-TYCZNY

692. Where is there a good barber?
Gdzie jest dobry fryzjer?
g-DZHEH yest DOHB-rih FRIZ-yehr?

693. I want a (haircut, shave).
Chcę się (ostrzyc, ogolić).
h-TSEH sheh (OHST-chits, oh-GOH-leech).

694. Not too short.
Nie za krótko.
nyeh zah KROOT-koh.

695. I part my hair on the side.
Czeszę się na przedział.
CHEH-sheh sheh nah PSHEH-dzhow.

696. In the middle.
Po środku.
poh SHROHD-koo.

697. The water is too (hot, cold).
Woda jest za (gorąca, zimna).
VOH-dah yest zah (goh-RON-tsah, ZHEEM-nah).

698. I want my shoes shined.
Proszę mi wyczyścić buty.
PROH-sheh mee vih-CHISH-cheech BOO-tih.

699. Can I make an appointment for ——?
Czy mogę zamówić godzinę ——?
chih MOH-geh zah-MOO-veech goh-DZHEE-neh ——?

700. I want a shampoo.
Chcę umyć głowę.
h-TSEH OO-mich GWOH-veh.

701. A finger wave. 702. A permanent.

Układanie włosów. Wieczna ondulacja.

ook-wah-DAH-nyeh VWOH-soov. VYECH-nah ohn-doo-LAHTS-yah.

703. A manicure.

Manicure.

mah-NEE-keer.

PHOTOGRAPHY
FOTOGRAFOWANIE

706. I want a roll of (color) film.

Proszę o rolkę (kolorowego) filmu.

PROH-sheh oh ROHL-keh (koh-loh-roh-VEH-goh) FEEL-mo.

707. The size is ——.

Rozmiar: ——.

ROHZ-myahr: ——.

708. Movie film. 709. For this camera.

Film dla aparatu filmowego. Do tego aparatu.

feelm dla ah-pah-RAH-too feel-moh-VEH-goh. doh TEH-goh ah-pah-RAH-too.

710. What is the charge for developing a roll?

Illę kosztuje wywołanie filmu?

EE-leh kosh-TOO-yeh vih-voh-WAH-nyeh FEEL-moo?

711. For one print of each.

Jedna odbitka z każdego.

YED-nah ohd-BEET-kah z kahzh-DEH-goh.

712. For an enlargement.

Powiększanie.

poh-vyen-KSHAH-nyeh.

713. The camera is out of order.

Aparat się zepsuł.

ah-PAH-raht sheh ZEP-sool.

714. When will they be ready?

Kiedy będą gotowe?

KYEH-dih BEN-dohn goh-TOH-veh?

715. Do you rent cameras?

Czy pan wypożycza aparaty fotograficzne?

chih pahn vih-poh-ZHIH-chah ah-pah-RAH-tih foh-toh-grah-FEECH-neh?

716. I should like one for today.

Chciałbym aparat na dzisiaj.

h-CHOW-bim ah-PAH-raht nah DZHEE-shie.

LAUNDRY AND DRY CLEANING
PRALNIA I CZYSZCZENIE CHEMICZNE

719. Where is the nearest (laundry, dry cleaner)?

Gdzie jest najbliższa pralnia?

g-DZHEH yest nie-BLEEZH-shah PRAHL-nyah?

720. To be (washed, mended).

Proszę (uprać, zacerować).

PROH-sheh (OOP-rahch, zah-tseh-ROH-vahch).

721. (**Cleaned, pressed**).

(Wyczyścić, uprasować).

vih-CHISH-cheech, oop-rah-SOH-vahch).

722. Do not wash this in hot water.

Proszę nie prać tego w gorącej wodzie.

*PROH-sheh nyeh prahch TEH-goh v goh-
ROHN-tsay VOH-dzheh.*

723. Use lukewarm water.

Proszę użyć letnią wodę.

PROH-sheh OO-zhih LET-nyoh VOH-deh.

724. Be very careful.

Bardzo ostrożnie, proszę.

*BAHRD-zoh ohs-TROHZH-nyeh, PROH-
sheh.*

725. Do not dry this in the sun.

Proszę nie suszyć tego na słońcu.

*PROH-sheh nyeh SOO-shich TEH-goh nah
SWOHN-tsoo.*

726. (**Do not**) **starch the collars.**

Proszę (nie) krochmalić kołnierzy.

*PROH-sheh (nyeh) kroh-MAH-leech kohw-
NYEH-zhih.*

727. When can I have this?

Kiedy będzie gotowe?

KYEH-dih BEN-dzheh goh-TOH-veh?

728. Here is the list.

Tutaj jest spis.

TOO-tie yest speess.

729. The belt is missing.

Pasek został zgubiony.

PAH-sek ZOH-stow zgoo-BYOH-nih.

See also CLOTHING

CLOTHING
ODZIEŻ

731. Apron.   732. Bathing cap.
733. Bathing suit.

Fartuch.   Czepek kąpielowy.   Kostium
    kąpielowy.

FAR-tooh.   CHEH-pek kohm-pyeh-LOH-vih.
    KOHST-yoom kohm-pyeh-LOH-vih.

734. Blouse.   735. Brassiere.   736. Coat.

Bluzka.   Stanik.   Palto.

BLOOS-kah.   STAH-neek.   PAHL-toh.

737. Collar.   738. Diapers.   739. Dress.

Kołnierz.   Pieluszki.   Suknia.

KOHN-nyezh.   pyeh-LOOSH-kee.   SOOK-
    nyah.

740. Garters.   741. Gloves.

Podwiązki.   Rękawiczki.

pohd-VYOHN-skee.   ren-kah-VEECH-kee.

742. Handkerchief.   743. Hat.
744. Jacket.

Chusteczka.   Kapelusz.   Kurtka.

hoos-TECH-kah.   kah-PEH-loosh.   KOORT-
    kah.

745. Necktie.   746. Nightgown.
747. Overcoat.

Krawat.   Koszula Nocna.   Płaszcz.
KRAH-vaht.   koh-SHOO-lah   NOHTS-nah.
pwahshch.

748. Pajamas.   749. Panties.   750. Petticoat.

Piżama.   Majtki.   Halka.
pee-ZHAH-mah.   MIET-kee.   HAHL-kah.

751. Raincoat.   752. Riding clothes.

Płaszcz deszczowy.   Ubranie do konnej
jazdy.
*PWAHSH-ch   desh-CHOH-vih.   oob-RAH-
nyeh doh KOHN-nay YAHZ-dih.*

753. Robe.   754. Shirt.   755. Shorts.

Szlafrok.   Koszula.   Kalesony.
*SHLAH-frohk.   koh-SHOO-lah.   kah-leh-
SOH-nih.*

756. Undershirt.   757. Slip.

Podkoszulka.   Koszula damska.
*pohd-koh-SHOOL-kah.   koh-SHOO-lah
DAHMS-kah.*

758. Slippers.   759. Socks.

Pantofle ranne.   Skarpetki.
pahn-TOH-fleh RAHN-neh.   skahr-PET-kee.

760. Nylon stockings.   761. Suit.

Nylonowe pończochy.   Kostium.
*nie-loh-NOH-veh pohn-CHOH-khih. KOHST-
yoom.*

**762. Suspenders.   763. Sweater.
764. Trousers.**

Szelki. Sweter. Spodnie.
SHEL-kee. SVEH-ter. SPOHD-nyeh.

765. Underwear.   766. Vest.

Bielizna. Kamizelka.
byeh-LEEZ-nah. kah-mee-ZEL-kah.

HEALTH AND ACCIDENTS
ZDROWIE I WYPADKI

769. There has been an accident.

Zdarzył się nieszczęśliwy wypadek.
*ZDAH-zhil sheh nyehsh-chen-SHLEE-vih vih-
PAH-dek.*

770. Get a (doctor, nurse).

Proszę zawołać (doktora, pielęgniarkę).
*PROH-sheh   zah-VOH-wahch   (dohk-TOH-
rah, pyeh-leng-NYAHR-keh).*

771. Send for an ambulance.

Proszę posłać po pogotowie ratunkowe.
*PROH-sheh POHS-wahch poh poh-go-toh-vyeh
rah-toon-KOH-veh.*

772. Please bring blankets.

Proszę przynieść koc.
PROH-sheh PSHIH-nyesh-ch KOH-ts.

773. A stretcher.   Water.

Nosze. Woda.
NOH-sheh. VOH-dah.

774. He is (seriously) injured.
Jest (poważnie) ranny.
yest (poh-VAHZH-nyeh) RAHN-nih.

775. Help me carry him.
Proszę mi pomóc go przenieść.
PROH-sheh mee POH-moots goh PSHEH-nyesh-ch.

776. He was knocked down.
Został zwalony z nóg.
ZOHS-tow zvah-LOH-nih z noog.

777. She has (fallen, fainted).
(Upadła, zemdlała).
(oo-PAHD-wah, zem-DLAH-wah).

778. I feel faint.
Słabo mi.
SWAH-boh mee.

779. Fracture. Bruise. Cut.
Złamanie. Stłuczenie. Ranka.
zwah-MAH-nyeh. stwoo-CHEH-nyeh. RAHN-kah.

780. He has (burned, cut) his hand.
On (oparzył, zranił) rękę.
ohn (oh-PAH-zhill, ZRAH-nill) REN-keh.

781. Can you dress this?
(to M.) Czy pan może to opatrzyć?
chih pahn MOH-zheh toh oh-PAHT-shich?

782. Have you any (bandages, splints)?
(to M.) Czy pan ma (bandaże, łupki)?
chih pahn mah (bahn-DAH-zheh, WOOP-kee)?

783. Are you all right?
(to M.) Czy pan się dobrze czuje?
chih pahn sheh DOHB-zheh CHOO-yeh?

784. It hurts here.
Tu mnie boli.
too-mn-YEH BOH-lee.

785. I want to sit down a moment.
Chcę usiąść na chwilę.
kh-TSEH OO-shohnsh-ch nah HVEE-leh.

786. I cannot move my ——.
Nie mogę ruszać mojej ——.
nyeh MOH-geh ROO-shahch MOH-yay ——.

787. I have hurt my ——.
Uraziłem moją ——.
oo-rah-ZHEE-wem MOH-yohn ——.

See also PARTS OF THE BODY

790. Can I travel on Monday?
Czy będę mógł jechać w poniedziałek?
chih BEN-deh moogll YEH-hahch v poh-nyeh-DZHAH-wek?

791. Please notify my (husband, wife).
Proszę zawiadomić (mojego męża, moją żonę).
PROH-sheh zah-vyah-DOH-meech (moh-YEH-goh MEN-zhah, MOH-yohn ZHOH-neh).

792. Here is my identification.
Tu jest moja legitymacja.
tu yest MOH-yah leh-gee-tih-MAHTS-yah.

ILLNESS
CHOROBA

795. **I wish to see a (doctor, specialist).**
Chcę pójść do (doktora, specjalisty).
*h-TSEH poo-EESH-ch doh (dohk-TOH-rah,
spets-yah-LEES-tih).*

796. **An American doctor.**
Amerykański doktór.
ah-meh-rih-KAHN-skee DOHK-toor.

797. **I do not sleep well.**
Nie śpię dobrze.
nyeh sh-PYEH DOHB-zheh.

798. **My foot hurts.**
Stopa mnie boli.
STOH-pah mn-YEH BOH-lee.

799. **My head aches.**
Głowa mnie boli.
GWOH-vah mn-YEH BOH-lee.

800. **I have an abscess.**
Mam wrzód.
mahm vzhood.

801. **Appendicitis.   Biliousness.**
Wyrostek robaczkowy.   Mdłości.
*vih-ROHS-tek roh-bahch-KOH-vih.
MDWOSH-chee.*

802. **A blister.**
Otarcie.
oh-TAHR-cheh.

803. A boil.   804. A burn.
Furunkuł.   Sparzenie.
foo-ROON-kool.   spah-ZHE-nyeh.

805. Chills.   806. A cold.
Dreszcze.   Przeziębienie.
DRESH-cheh.   pshe-zhen-BYEN-nyeh.

807. Constipation.   808. A cough.
Obstrukcja.   Kaszel.
ohbs-TROOK-tsyah.   KAH-shel.

809. A cramp.   810. Diarrhœa.
Skurcz.   Biegunka.
skoorch.   byeh-GOON-kah.

811. Dysentery.   812. An earache.
Dyzenteria.   Ból ucha.
dih-zen-TER-yah.   bool OO-khah.

813. A fever.   814. Food poisoning.
Gorączka.   Zatrucie żołądka.
*goh-ROHNCH-kah.   zah-TROO-cheh zhoh-
WOHND-kah.*

815. Hoarseness.   816. Indigestion.
Chrypka.   Niestrawność.
KHRIP-kah.   nyeh-STRAHV-nohsh-ch.

817. Nausea.   818. Pneumonia.
Nudności.   Zapalenie płuc.
*nood-NOHSH-chee.   zah-pah-LEH-nyeh
pwoots.*

819. A sore throat.   820. Sore.
Ból gardła.   Ranka.
bool GAHRD-wah.   RAHN-kah.

821. Chafed.   822. A sprain.
Otarcie.   Nadwyrężenie.
oh-TAHR-cheh.   nahd-vih-ren-ZHEH-nyeh.

823. Sunstroke.
Porażenie słoneczne.
poh-rah-ZHEH-nyeh.   swoh-NECH-neh.

824. Typhoid fever.   825. To vomit.
Tyfus.   Wymiotować.
TIH-foos.   vih-myoh-TOH-vahch.

826. What am I to do?
Co mam robić?
tsoh mahm ROH-beech?

827. Must I stay in bed?
Czy muszę leżeć w łóżku?
chih MOO-sheh LEH-zhech v WOOZH-koo?

828. Do I have to go to a hospital?
Czy muszę iść do szpitala?
chih MOO-sheh EESH-ch doh shpee-TAH-lah?

829. May I get up?
Czy mogę wstać?
chih MOH-geh vstahch?

830. I feel better.
Czuję się lepiej.
CHOO-yeh sheh LEP-yay.

831. When do you think I'll be better?
Kiedy będę się czuł lepiej?
KYEH-dih BEN-deh sheh chool LEP-yay?

832. When will you come again?
(to M.) Kiedy pan przyjdzie znowu?
KYEH-dih pahn PSHIH-ee-dzheh ZNOH-voo?

833. A drop. 834. A teaspoonful.
Kropla. Łyżeczka.
KROHP-lah. wih-ZHECH-kah.

835. Hot water. 836. Ice. 837. Medicine.
Gorąca woda. Lód. Lekarstwo.
goh-RON-tsah VOH-dah. lood. leh-KAHRST-voh.

838. A pill. 839. Prescription.
Pigułka. Recepta.
pee-GOOLL-kah. reh-TSEP-tah.

840. Every hour. 841. (Before, after) meals.
Co godzinę. (Przed, po) jedzeniu.
tsoh goh-DZHEE-neh. (pshed, poh) yeh-DZEH-nyoo.

842. Twice a day.
Dwa razy dziennie.
dvah RAH-zih DZHEN-nyeh.

843. On going to bed. 844. On getting up.
Przed pójściem do łóżka. Z rana.
pshed poo-EESH-chem doh WOOZH-kah. z RAH-nah.

845. X-ray.
Prześwietlenie.
pshesh-vyet-LEH-nyeh.

See also DRUGSTORE.

DENTIST
DENTYSTA

850. Do you know a good dentist?

Proszę polecić dobrego dentystę.

PROH-sheh poh-LEH-cheech doh-BREH-goh den-TIS-teh.

851. This (front, back) tooth hurts.

(Przedni, tylny) ząb mnie boli.

(PSHED-nee, TIL-nih) zohmb mn-YEH BOH-lee.

852. Can you fix it (temporarily)?

(*to M.*) Czy pan może zaleczyć (tymczasowo)?

chih pahm MOH-zheh zah-LEH-chich (tim-chah-SOH-voh)?

853. I have lost a filling.

Zgubiłem plombę.

zgoo-BEE-wehm PLOHM-beh.

854. I (do not) want it extracted.

Proszę (nie) wyrwać.

PROH-sheh (nyeh) VIHR-vahch.

855. Can you repair this bridge?

(*to M.*) Czy pan może naprawić ten mostek?

chih pahn MOH-zheh nah-PRAH-veech ten MOHST-ek?

DRUG STORE
APTEKA

857. Where is there a drug store where they understand English?

Gdzie jest apteka, gdzie mówią po angielsku?

g-DŻHEH jest ahp-TEH-kah, g-DŻHEH MOO-vyon poh ahn-GYEL-skoo?

858. Can you fill a prescription?

(*to M.*) Czy pan może przygotować receptę?

chih pahn MOH-zheh pshih-goh-TOH-vahch reh-TSEP-teh?

859. How long will it take?

Jak długo będzie trwało?

yahk DWOO-goh BEN-dzheh TRVAH-woh?

860. I want adhesive tape.

Proszę o plaster.

PROH-sheh oh PLAHS-ter.

**861. Alcohol. 862. Antiseptic.
863. Aspirin.**

Alkohol. Antyseptyk. Aspiryna.

ahl-KOH-hol. ahn-tih-SEP-tik. ahs-pee-RIH-nah.

864. Bandages.

Bandaże.

bahn-DAH-zheh.

865. Bicarbonate of soda.

Soda oczyszczona.

SOH-dah oh-chish-CHOH-nah.

866. Boric acid. 867. A (hair, tooth) brush.
Kwas borny. Szczotka do (włosów,
zębów).
*kvahs BOR-nih. sh-CHOHT-kah doh
(VWOH-soov, ZEM-boov).*

868. Carbolic acid. 869. Castor oil.
Kwas karbolowy. Rycyna.
kvahs kahr-boh-LOH-vih. rih-TSIH-nah.

870. Cleaning fluid. 871. Cold cream.
Płyn do czyszczenia. Krem.
puin do chish-CHEH-nyah. krem.

**872. A comb. 873. Corn pads.
874. Cotton.**
Grzebień. Plaster do odcisków. Wata.
*GZHEH-byehn. PLAHS-ter doh ohd-
CHEES-koov. VAH-tah.*

**875. An eye cup. 876. Foot powder.
877. Gauze. 878. Hair tonic.**
Wanienka do oka. Puder do nóg.
Gaza. Pomada do włosow.
*vah-NYEN-kah doh OH-kah. POO-der doh
noog. GAH-zah. poh-MAH-dah doh
VWOH-soov.*

879. A hot water bottle. 880. An ice bag.
Flaszka z gorącą wodą. Woreczek do
lodu.
*FLAHSH-kah z goh-RON-tsoh VOH-doh.
voh-REH-chek doh LOH-doo.*

881. Iodine.   882. A laxative.

Jodyna.   Środek na przeczyszczenie.

yoh-DIH-nah.   S̄HROH-dek nah psheh-chish-CHEH-nyeh.

883. Lipstick.   884. A medicine dropper.

Pomadka do ust.   Pipetka.

poh-MAHD-kah doh oost.   pee-PEHT-kah.

885. A mouthwash.   886. Peroxide.

Woda do zębów.   Woda utleniona.

VOH-dah doh ZEM-boov.   VOH-dah oot-leh-NYOH-nah.

887. Poison.   888. Powder.   889. Quinine.

Trucizna.   Puder.   Chinina.

troo-C̄HEEZ-nah.   POO-der.   khee-NEE-nah.

890. A razor.   891. Razor blade.

Brzytwa.   Żyletka.

BZHIT-vah.   zhih-LET-kah.

892. Rouge.

Róz.

roozh.

893. A sedative (liquid, cream).

Środek nasenny (płyn, krem).

S̄HROH-dehk nah-SEN-nih (pwin, krem).

894. Shaving lotion.   895. Shaving cream.

Woda po goleniu.   Krem do golenia.

VOH-dah poh goh-LEH-nyoo.   KREM doh goh-LEH-nyah.

896. Soap.   897. Sunburn ointment.
Mydło.   Krem do opalania.
MID-woh.   krem doh oh-pah-LAH-nyah.

898. Suntan oil.   899. Thermometer.
Olejek przeciwsłoneczny.   Termometr.
oh-LEH-yek psheh-cheev-swoh-NECH-nih. ter
   MOH-metr.

900. Tooth (paste, powder).
(Pasta, proszek) do zębów.
(PAHS-tah, PROH-shek) doh ZEM-boov.

PARTS OF THE BODY
CZĘŚCI CIAŁA

902. The ankle.   903. The appendix.
Kostka.   Wyrostek robaczkowy.
KOHST-kah.   vih-ROS-tek roh-bahch-KOH-
   vih.

904. The arm.   905. The back.   906. The
   blood.
Ramię.   Plecy.   Krew.
RAH-myeh.   PLEH-tsih.   krev.

907. The bone.   908. The cheek.   909. The
   chest.
Kość.   Policzek.   Piersi.
KOHSH-ch.   poh-LEE-chek.   PYER-shee.

910. The chin.   911. The collar bone.
Podbródek.   Obojczyk.
pohd-BROO-dek.   oh-BOY-chik.

912. The ear.   913. The elbow.
Ucho.   Łokieć.
OO-khoh.   WOH-kyech.

914. The eye.   915. The eyebrows.
916. The eyelashes.
Oko.   Brwi.   Rzęsy.
OH-koh.   br-VEE.   ZHEN-sih.

917. The eyelid.   918. The face.
919. The finger.
Powieka.   Twarz.   Palec.
poh-VYEH-kah.   tvahzh.   PAH-lets.

920. The foot.   921. The forehead.
Stopa.   Czoło.
STOH-pah.   CHOH-woh.

922. The hair.   923. The hand.
Włosy.   Ręka.
VWOH-sih.   REN-kah.

924. The head.   925. The heart.
Głowa.   Serce.
GWOH-vah.   SER-tseh.

926. The heel.   927. The hip.
Pięta.   Biodro.
PYEN-ta.   BYOHD-roh.

928. The intestines.   929. The jaw.
Wnętrzności.   Szczęka.
vnen-TSHNOHSH-chee.   sh-CHEN-kah.

930. The joint.   931. The kidney.
Staw.   Nerka.
stahv.   NER-kah.

**932. The knee.   933. The leg.
934. The lip.**
Kolano. Noga. Warga.
koh-LAH-noh.   NOH-gah.   VAHR-gah.

935. The liver.   936. The lung.
Wątroba. Płuco.
wohn-TROH-bah.   PWOO-tsoh.

937. The mouth.   938. The muscle.
Usta. Mięsień.
OOS-tah.   MYEN-shen.

**939. The nail.   940. The neck.
941. The nerve.**
Paznokieć. Szyja. Nerw.
pahz-NOH-kyech.   SHIH-yah.   nerv.

942. The nose.   943. The rib.
Nos. Żebro.
nohs.   ZEHB-roh.

**944. The shoulders.   945. The (right, left)
side.**
Barki. (Prawa, lewa) strona.
*BAHR-kee.   (PRAH-vah,   LEH-vah)
STROH-nah.*

946. The skin.   947. The skull.
Skóra. Czaszka.
SKOO-rah.   CHAHSH-kah.

948. The spine.   949. The stomach.
Kręgosłup. Żołądek.
kren-GOH-swoop.   zhoh-WOHN-dek.

950. The tooth.   951. The thigh.

Ząb. Udo.

zomb.   OO-doh.

952. The throat.   953. The thumb.

Gardło. Kciuk.

GAHR-dwoh. KC̄H-ook.

954. The toe.   955. The tongue.

Palec u nogi. Język.

PAH-lets oo NOH-gee.   YEN-zik.

956. The tonsils.   957. The waist.
958. The wrist.

Migdały. Talia. Przegub.

meeg-DAH-wih.   TAH-lyah.   PSHEH-goob.

COMMUNICATIONS: TELEPHONE
KOMUNIKACJA: TELEFON

960. Where can I telephone?

Skąd mogę zatelefonować?

skond MOH-geh zah-teh-leh-foh-NOH-vahc̄h?

961. Will you telephone for me?

(*to M.*) Czy może pan zatelefonować za
mnie?

*chih MOH-zhe pahn zah-teh-leh-foh-NOH-
vahc̄h zah mn-YEH?*

962. I want to make a local call to ——.

Chcę zatelefonować do ——.

h-TSEH zah-teh-leh-foh-NOH-vahc̄h doh

963. A long distance call.
Dlugo dystansowa rozmowa.
DWOO-goh dis-tahn-SOH-vah rohz-MOH-vah.

964. The operator will call you.
Telefonistka zadzwoni.
teh-leh-foh-NEEST-kah zahdz-VOH-nee.

965. I want number ——.
Chcę numer ——.
h-TSEH NOO-mer ——.

966. Hello.
Halo.
HAH-loh.

967. They do not answer.
Nie odpowiadają.
nyeh ohd-poh-vyah-DAH-yoh.

968. The line is busy.
Linia zajęta.
LEEN-yah zah-YEN-tah.

969. May I speak to ——?
Czy mogę mówić z ——?
chih MOH-geh MOO-veech z ——?

970. He is not in.
Jego niema w domu.
YEH-goh NYEH-mah v DOH-moo.

971. This is —— speaking.
Tu mówi ——.
too MOO-vee ——.

972. Please take a message for ――.

Proszę przyjąć polecenie dla ――.

PROH-sheh PSHIH-yonch̄ poh-leh-TSEH-nyeh dlah ――.

973. My number is ――.

Mój numer jest ――.

MOO-ee NOO-mer yest ――.

974. How much is a call to ――?

Ile kosztuje rozmowa do ――?

EE-leh kosh-TOO-yeh rohz-MOH-vah doh ――?

975. There is a telephone call for you.

(*to M.*) Wołają pana do telefonu.

voh-WAH-yoh PAH-nah doh teh-leh-FOH-noo.

TELEGRAMS AND CABLEGRAMS
TELEGRAMY I KABLOGRAMY

977. Where can I send a (telegram, cablegram)?

Gdzie mogę nadać (telegram, kablogram)?

g-DZ̄HEH MOH-geh NAH-dahch̄ (teh-LEH-grahm, kah-BLOH-grahm)?

978. What is the rate per word to ――?

Ile kosztuje jedno słowo do ――?

EE-leh kosh-TOO-yeh YED-noh SWOH-voh doh ――?

979. Where are the forms?

Gdzie są formularze?

g-DZ̄HEH sohn for-moo-LAH-sheh?

980. Urgent.   When will it arrive?
Pilne.   Kiedy to dojdzie?
PEEL-neh.   KYEH-dih toh DOH-ee-dzheh?

981. I wish to pay for the answer.
Chcę opłacić odpowiedź.
h-TSEH ohp-WAH-cheech ohd-POH-vyedzh.

USEFUL INFORMATION: DAYS OF THE WEEK
DNI TYGODNIA

883. Sunday.
Niedziela.
nyeh-DZHEH-lah.

984. Monday.   Tuesday.
Poniedziałek.   Wtorek.
poh-nyeh-DZHAH-wek.   VTOH-rek.

985. Wednesday.   Thursday.
Środa.   Czwartek.
SHROH-dah.   CHVAHR-tek.

986. Friday.   Saturday.
Piątek.   Sobota.
PYOHN-tek.   soh-BOH-tah.

MONTHS, SEASONS AND WEATHER
MIESIĄCE, PORY ROKU I POGODA

987. January.   February.
Styczeń.   Luty.
STIH-chen.   LOO-tih.

988. March.   April.
Marzec.   Kwiecień.
MAH-zhets.   KVYEH-chen.

989. May.   June.
Maj.   Czerwiec.
mie.   CHER-vyets.

990. July.   August.
Lipiec.   Sierpien.
LEEP-yets.   SHER-pyen.

991. September.   October.
Wrzesien.   Październik.
VZHEH-shen.   pahzh-DZHER-neek.

992. November.   December.
Listopad.   Grudzień.
lees-TOH-pahd.   GROO-dzhen.

993. Spring.   Summer.
Wiosna.   Lato.
VYOHS-nah.   LAH-toh.

994. Autumn.   Winter.
Jesień.   Zima.
YEH-shen.   ZHEE-mah.

995. It is (warm, cold).
Jest (ciepło, zimno).
yest (CHEP-woh, ZHEEM-noh).

996. It is (fair, good, bad).
Jest (pogodnie, dobrze, źle).
yest poh-GOHD-nyeh, DOHB-zheh, zhleh).

997. It is (raining, snowing).
Pada (deszcz, śnieg).
PAH-dah (DESH-ch, shnyeg).

998. The sun. Sunny. The shade.
Słonce. Słonecznie. Cień.
SWOHN-tseh. swoh-NECH-nyeh. chen.

TIME AND TIME EXPRESSIONS
CZAS

1000. What time is it?
Która godzina?
KTOO-rah goh-DZHEE-nah?

1001. It is two o'clock (A.M., P.M.).
Jest druga godzina (rano, po południu).
yest DROO-gah goh-DZHEE-nah (RAH-noh, poh poh-WOOD-nyoo).

1002. It is thirty minutes to ——.
Jest pół do ——.
yest pooll doh ——.

1003. It is a quarter past ——.
Jest kwadrans po ——.
yest KVAHD-rahns poh ——.

1004. It is a quarter to ——.
Jest kwadrans do ——.
yest KVAHD-rahns doh ——.

1005. At ten minutes to ——.
Za dziesięć ——.
zah DZHEH-shench ——.

1006. At ten minutes past ——.
Dziesięć po ——.
DZHEH-shench poh ——.

1007. In the morning.   In the evening.
Rano.   Wieczór.
RAH-no.   VYEH-choor.

1008. In the afternoon.   At noon.
Po południu.   W południe.
poh poh-WOOD-nyoo.   v poh-WOOD-nyeh.

1009. Day.   Night.   Midnight.
Dzień.   Noc.   Północ.
dzhen.   nohts.   POOW-nohts.

1010. Yesterday.   Last night.
Wczoraj.   Wczoraj wieczorem.
VCHOH-rie.   vchoh-rie vyeh-CHOH-rem.

1011. Today.   Tonight.   Tomorrow.
Dzisiaj.   Dzisiaj wieczorem.   Jutro.
DZHEE-shie.   DZHEE-shie vyeh-CHOH-rem.   YOOT-roh.

1012. The day before yesterday.
Przedwczoraj.
pshed-VCHOH-rie.

1013. Last year.   Last month.
Zeszłego roku.   Zeszłego miesiąca.
zesh-WEH-goh ROH-koo.   zesh-WEH-goh myeh-SHOHN-tsah.

1014. Next Monday. Next week.
Następny poniedziałek. Następny tydzień.
nahs-TEMP-nih poh-nyeh-DZ̲HAH-wek.
nahs-TEMP-nih TIH-dz̲hen.

1015. Two weeks ago.
Dwa tygodnie temu.
dvah tih-GOHD-nyeh TEH-moo.

NUMBERS

1016. One. Two. Three.
Jeden. Dwa. Trzy.
YEH-den. dvah. tshih.

1017. Four. Five. Six.
Cztery. Pięć. Sześć.
CHTEH-rih. pyehn-ch̄. shensh̄-c̄h̄.

1018. Seven. Eight. Nine.
Siedem. Osiem. Dziewięć.
S̄HEH-dem. OH-shehm. DZ̲HEH-vehnc̄h̄.

1019. Ten. Eleven. Twelve.
Dziesięć. Jedynaście. Dwanaście.
DZ̲HEH-shenc̄h̄. yeh-dih-ṆASH-c̄heh.
dvah-NAS̄H̄-c̄heh.

1020. Thirteen. Fourteen. Fifteen.
Trzynaście. Czternaście. Piętnaście.
tshih-NAS̄H̄-c̄heh. chtehr-NAHS̄H̄-c̄heh.
pyehnt-NAHS̄H̄-c̄heh.

1021. Sixteen. Seventeen. Eighteen.
Szesnaście. Siedemnaście. Osiemnaście.
shehs-NAHSH-cheh.　sheh-dem-NAHSH-cheh.　oh-shehm-NAHSH-cheh.

1022. Nineteen. Twenty. Twenty-one.
Dziewiętnaście. Dwadzieścia. Dwadzieścia jeden.
dzheh-vyehnt-NAHSH-cheh.　dvah-DZHESH-chah.　dvah-DZHEHSH-chah YEH-den.

1023. Twenty-two. Thirty. Thirty-one.
Dwadzieścia dwa. Trzydzieści. Trzydzieści jeden.
dvah-DZHEHSH-chah　dvah.　tshih-DZHESH-chih.　tshih-DZHEHSH-chih YEH-den.

1024. Forty. Fifty. Sixty.
Czterdzieści. Pięćdziesiąt. Sześćdziesiąt.
chtehr-DZHEHSH-chih.　pyehnch-DZHEH-shohnt.　shehsh-ch-DZHEH-shohnt.

1025. Seventy. Eighty. Ninety.
Siedemdziesiąt. Osiemdziesiąt. Dziewięćdziesiąt.
sheh-dem-DZEH-shohnt.　oh-shehm-DZHEH-shohnt.　dzheh-vyehnt-DZHEH-shohnt.

1026. One hundred. One hundred and one.
Sto. Sto jeden.
stoh.　stoh YEH-den.

**1027. Two hundred. One thousand. Two
thousand.**
Dwieście. Tysiąc. Dwa tysiące.
*DVYEHSH-cheh. TIH-shohn-ts. dvah tih-
SHOHN-tseh.*

1028. One million.
Milion.
MEEL-yohn.

1029. 1956.
Tysiąc dziewięćset pięćdziesiąt sześć.
*TIH-shohn-ts dzheh-WYEHNT-set pyehnch-
DZHEH-shohnt schensh-ch.*

1030. First. Second. Third.
Pierwszy. Drugi. Trzeci.
PYEHR-vshih. DROO-gee. TSHEH-chee.

1031. Fourth. Fifth. Sixth.
Czwarty. Piąty. Szósty.
CHVAHR-tih. PYOHN-tih. SHOOS-tih.

1032. Seventh. Eighth. Ninth.
Siódmy. Ósmy. Dziewiąty.
SHOOD-mih. OOS-mih. dzheh-VOHN-tih

1033. Tenth. Eleventh. Twelfth.
Dziesiąty. Jedynasty. Dwunasty.
*dzheh-SHOHN-tih.   yeh-dih-NAHS-tih.
dvoo-NAHS-tih.*

**1034. Twentieth. Thirtieth. One
hundredth.**
Dwudziesty. Trzydziesty. Setny.
*dvoo-DZHEHS-tih.   tshih-DZHEHS-tih.
SET-nih.*

MEASUREMENTS

1035. What is the (length, width)?

Jaka (długość, szerokość)?

YAH-kah (DWOO-gosh-ch̄, sheh-ROH-kosh-ch̄)?

1036. How much is it per meter?

Ile kosztuje metr?

EE-leh kosh-TOO-yeh metr?

1037. What is the size?

Jaki rozmiar?

YAH-kee ROHZ-myahr?

1038. It is ten meters long by four meters wide.

Jest dziesięć metrów długie i cztery metry szerokie.

yest DZHEH-shench MET-roov DWOO-gyeh ee ch-TEH-rih MET-rih sheh-ROH-kyeh.

1039. High. Low.

Wysoko. Nisko.

vih-SOH-koh. NEES-koh.

1040. Large. Small. Medium.

Duże. Małe. Średnie.

DOO-zheh. MAH-weh. SHRED-nyeh.

1041. Alike. Different.

Jednakowe. Różne.

yed-nah-KOH-veh. ROOZH-neh.

1042. A pair. A dozen.
Para. Tuzin.
PAH-rah. TOO-z̄heen.

1043. Half a dozen.
Pół tuzina.
pooll too-Z̄HEE-nah.

1044. Half a meter.
Pół metra.
pooll MET-rah.

COLORS
KOLORY

1047. Light. Dark.
Jasny. Ciemny.
YAHS-nih. C̄HEM-nih.

1048. Black. Blue. Brown.
Czarny. Niebieski. Brązowy.
CHAHR-nih. nyeh-BYEH-skee. brohn-Z̄OH-vih.

1049. Cream. Gray. Green.
Kremowy. Szary. Zielony.
krem-OH-vih. SHAH-rih. z̄he-LOH-nih.

1050. Orange. Pink. Violet.
Pomarańczowy. Różowy. Fioletowy.
poh-mah-rahn̄-CHOH-vih. roo-Z̄HOH-vih. fyoh-leh-TOH-vih.

1051. Red. White. Yellow.
Czerwony. Biały. żółty.
cher-VOH-nih. BYAH-wih. Z̄HOOW-tih.

1052. I want a (lighter, darker) shade.
Chcę (jaśniejszy, ciemniejszy) odcień.
h-TSEH (yahsh-NYAY-shih, chem-NYAH-shih) OHD-chen.

COMMON OBJECTS
PRZEDMIOTY CODZIENNEGO UŻYTKU

1055. Ash tray.   1056. A handbag.
Popielniczka.   Torebka.
poh-pyell-NEECH-kah.   toh-REB-kah.

1057. Boarding house.
Pensjonat.
pen-SYOH-naht.

1058. Bobby pins.   1059. A box.
Szpilki do włosów.   Skrzynka.
SHPEEL-kee doh VLOH-soov.   sk-SHIHN-kah.

1060. Candy.
Czekoladka.
cheh-koh-LAHD-kah.

1061. A can opener.
Klucz do otwierania puszek.
klooch doh oht-vyeh-RAH-nyah POO-shek.

1062. Cotton.   1063. Silk.   1064. Linen.
Bawełna.   Jedwab.   Płótno.
bah-VEL-nah.   YED-vahb.   PWOOT-noh.

1065. Wool.   1066. Cork.   1067. Corkscrew.
Wełna.   Korek.   Korkociąg.
VELL-nah.   KOH-rek.   kor-KOH-chong.

1068. Cushion. 1069. Doll. 1070. Earrings.
Poduszka. Lalka. Kolczyki.
poh-DOOSH-kah. LAL-kah. kol-CHIH-kee.

1071. Flashlight. 1072. Glasses.
Latarka elektryczna. Okulary.
lah-TAHR-kah eh-lek-TRICH-nah. oh-koo-LAH-rih.

1073. Sunglasses. 1074. Gold.
Okulary słoneczne. Złoto.
oh-koo-LAH-rih swoh-NECH-neh. ZWOH-toh.

1075. Chewing gum. 1076. Hair net.
Guma do żucia. Siatka do włosów.
GOO-mah doh ZHOO-chah. SHAHT-kah doh VWOH-soov.

1077. Hook. 1078. Flatiron. 1079. Jewelry.
Hak. Żelazko. Biżuteria.
hahk. zheh-LAHZ-koh. bee-zhoo-TER-yah.

1080. Shoelace. 1081. Leather.
Sznurowadło. Skóra.
shnoo-roh-VAHD-woh. SKOO-rah.

1082. Light bulb. 1083. Mending cotton.
Żarówka. Bawełna do cerowania.
zhah-ROOV-kah. bah-VELL-nah doh tse-roh-VAH-nyah.

1084. Net. 1085. Nail file.
Siatka. Pilnik do paznokci.
SHAHT-kah. PEEL-neek doh pahz-NOH-kchee.

1086. Necklace.   1087. Needle.
Naszyjnik.   Igła.
nah-SHIH-ee-neek.   EEG-wah.

1088. Notebook.   1089. Padlock.
Notatnik.   Kłódka.
noh-TAHT-neek.   KWOOD-kah.

1090. Pail.   1091. Penknife.
1092. Perfume.
Wiadro.   Nóż kieszonkowy.   Perfumy.
VYAHD-roh.   noozh kyeh-shon-KOH-vih.
per-FOO-mih.

1093. Pin (ornamental, straight).
Broszka.   Szpilka.
BROSH-kah.   SHPEEL-kah.

1094. Radio.   1095. Ring.   1096. Rubbers.
Radio.   Pierścionek.   Kalosze.
RAH-dyoh.   pyersh-CHOH-nek.   kah-LOH-
sheh.

1097. Safety pin.   1098. Scissors.
1099. Screw.
Agrafka.   Nożyczki.   Śruba.
ahg-RAHF-kah.   noh-ZHICH-kee.
SHROO-bah.

1100. Silver.   1101. Stone (precious).
Srebro.   Kamień (szlachetny).
SREB-roh.   KAH-myen (shlah-KHET-nih).

1102. Strap.
Pasek.
PAH-sek.

1103. Straw. 1104. Thimble. 1105. Thread.

Słomka. Naparstek. Nić.

SWOHM-kah. nah-PAHRS-tek. neech̄.

1106. Typewriter. 1107. Umbrella.
1108. Vase.

Maszyna do pisania. Parasol. Wazon.

mah-SHIH-nah doh pee-SAH-nyah. pah-RAH-sol. VAH-zohn.

1109. Watch. 1110. Whiskbroom.

Zegarek. Szczotka.

zeh-GAH-rek. sh-CHOT-kah.

1111. Wire. 1112. Wood. 1113. Wool
thread.

Drut. Drzewo. Nitka wełniana.

droot. DŻHEH-voh. NEET-kah vell-NYAH-nah.

1114. Zipper.

Zamek błyskawiczny.

ZAH-mek bwis-kah-VEECH-nih.

INDEX

The words in capitals refer to sections, and the first number that follows (example : p. 81) refers to the page. Otherwise, ALL ENTRIES ARE INDEXED BY ITEM NUMBER.